Black Robes, White Justice

BLACK ROBES, WHITE JUSTICE

by Bruce Wright

Lyle Stuart Inc.   *Secaucus, New Jersey*

Published by Lyle Stuart Inc.
120 Enterprise Ave., Secaucus, N.J. 07094
Published simultaneously in Canada by
Musson Book Company,
A division of General Publishing Co. Limited
Don Mills, Ontario

Address queries regarding rights and permissions
to Lyle Stuart Inc., 120 Enterprise Ave.,
Secaucus, N.J. 07094

Manufactured in the United States of America

Library of Congress Cataloging-in-Publication Data

Wright, Bruce, 1918—
    Black robes, white justice.

    1. Wright, Bruce, 1918—   . 2. Afro-American
judges—New York (N.Y.)—Biography. 3. Criminal
courts—New York (N.Y.) 4. Criminal justice,
Administration of—New York (N.Y.) 5. Race
discrimination—New York (N.Y.) I. Title.
KF373.W67A33   1987   345.73'05'08996073   87-9921
ISBN 0-8184-0422-1   347.305508996073

10   9   8   7   6

This book is for Patricia Fonville

Our laws make law impossible; our liberties destroy all freedom; our property is organized robbery; our morality is an impudent hypocrisy; our wisdom is administered by inexperienced or mal-experienced dupes; our power wielded by cowards and weaklings; and our honor false in all its points. I am an enemy of the existing order for good reasons. . . . The greatest of evils and the worst of crimes is poverty.

—George Bernard Shaw, Preface to *Major Barbara*

You wags that judge by rote, and damn by rule.

—Thomas Otway, Prologue to *Titus and Berenice*

Contents

Introduction

Professors and judges have, from time to time, written long and learned theses concerning the state of criminal law in America. These have ranged in their philosophic ferocity and anger from Karl Menninger's documentation of the crimes against criminals to J. Q. Wilson's suggestion that society simply lock up offenders and throw away the key. After ten turbulent years as a judge of New York City's Criminal Court, two more in Civil Court and now as a Supreme Court justice, I have elected to focus on this criminal justice system, if "justice" is the right word.

One of the tragedies of any criminal court occurs when it is reduced solely to a custodial conspiracy against those who break the law. The administrative structure of a large city's court system tempts the judges to dispose of the largest number of cases in the shortest period of time. Judges who accomplish this are said to be good "calendar people," and their rewards of preferment and promotion are examples to those who would otherwise pursue the vision of justice.

The quest for that moral force which is justice takes time. In trials and hearings, one must explore more than the meaning of enacted laws and the fact that they are said to have been breached. All kinds of complicated factors come into play. All too often, psychological questions arise to confront and vex our system of laws. Those of us called upon to sit in judgment of both laws and lawbreakers are not always qualified for such an onerous task. Most of the judges of America are male, white, middle-class, aloof and conservative. Brought before them is a parade of dark-skinned defendants, all alien to the concept the judges have of the way life ought to be.

In New York City, most judges have completed four years of college and three of law school. Presumably, such scholars are intellectuals of one kind or another. But more often than not, they are acquainted with no more than theories. Seldom do they have any personal familiarity with the reality and cruel adjectives which modify and diminish the lives of the poor. Such judges gaze upon the captives of the police across a vast expanse of social distance.

Idealists argue that one should always be tried before a jury of one's peers. No such elusive ethic troubles the vocation of judging. And yet, the urban nomads and peasants who make a territorial imperative of the streets are judged every day by those who are ignorant of and indifferent to the debased reality of those who are judged.

It is the pageant of the poor that concerns me, and the simultaneous but different ordeals of the judged and their judges, as each continues to confront the other.

My persistent concern has long been the white judges who, in their large numbers, are called upon daily to preside over the trials of black defendants accused of crime. Are they really qualified for such sociological tasks, only incidentally mixed with law? If so, what are the peculiar circumstances that define their competence? Is it the survival in them of some plantation concept of social divisions in life? What do they study in college or law school that might tend to qualify them to preside over the doom or liberty of strangers to their kinds of neighborhoods, of aliens to their way of life, of foreigners and outsiders to their clubs, their churches, their folkways? What magic abolishes color in their eyes and gives them instant objectivity and a license to analyze human foibles entirely divorced from the historical truth of racism? How, indeed, does one annul one's heritage and that of one's forefathers in this land or the land from which the family came?

Do white judges ever bring to bear a sober reflection on why there are so many black defendants in criminal cases? Do white judges ever wonder about why there are so few black lawyers appearing before them? Do they ever inquire about the history of bar associations that used to exclude Jews and blacks? Do they ever ponder aloud or in silence the reasons that there are so few black judges? Whenever I have raised the subject of bar association discrimination against blacks, my white colleagues profess never to have noticed any such thing.

For those of the inner city, as our dark enclaves are so euphemistically called, the judges are the assembly-line feeders of the prison system. Those in the system—whether prisoners, jailors or judges—who dare to speak of rehabilitation are regarded as wild-eyed speculators about the human spirit. They are accused of having more concern for the criminal than for the victims of crime. This abandonment of concepts of rehabilitation leads to society's preoccupation only with custody. This results in warehousing of offenders. The mean neighborhoods from which they come are neighborhoods transferred to the prisons. Little wonder that one black survivor of the inmate rebellion at Attica could weep an unanswered, perhaps unanswerable question to the world. "How the hell we gonna be *re*habilitated," he asked, "when we ain't never been *ha*bilitated in the first place?"

That so much urban crime is said to be the harsh mischief of blacks has caused the authoring of a great deal of supposition.

Some of it appears to be learned and earnest. Some gives way to emotion and presupposition.

Charles Silberman's book, *Criminal Violence: Criminal Justice*, suggests that blacks are hosts to a dreadful disease, a kind of innate violence. He describes this phenomenon as rather odd since, he says, it was not a part of their "baggage" when slaves were imported to this country. It almost allows a reader to believe that black Africans came to America as tourists. He ponders the way in which so many blacks seem isolated from and heedless of the behavior codes of the establishment. Yet he finds no evil consequence deriving from the history of black bondage in a democracy.

Silberman might be aided in the "analysis" of his menacing vision of black circumstance by a close reading of a small book by Anna Arnold Hedgeman. *The Gift of Chaos* is eloquent in its brevity. In one of her penetrating insights, Dr. Hedgeman writes that, at one time, blacks were the only immigrants to America who could never receive a letter or a package from home. They came without visas, without passports or tickets of passage.

In some societies, slavery has been quite usual, accepted as traditional. But America of the Colonists and the Founding Fathers had few historical canons it could call tradition. It did, however, have a Constitution which spoke grandly of liberty and equality. Under such a national charter black slavery became a nettlesome incongruity. It could only be explained in terms of a *believed* inferiority, a belief that both slave and master were supposed to have. Thus was shaped a national attitude.

The question of color has intruded at every step of a stumbling history. America's courts, where color should be irrelevant, have been little different from other segments of the nation's life. Color is more than an idle statistic; it is an enduring reality. It is America's way of life.

Some portions of this book may lead to accusations that will

14

reinforce the tensions that sadly exist between some blacks and some Jews. If so, then I will be misunderstood, because my belief that Jews and blacks should be natural allies in this white and Christian country is an abiding one. I ache for a reconciliation between the two groups, knowing that it seems painfully distant.

In portraying Jewish-black relations, I have tried to do so as though in the midst of a family dispute, with affectionate critical candor. I deplore anti-Semitism as I do any form of racism, whether expressed in private or publicly. At the same time, I have long felt that both Jews and blacks are an endangered species in this land of ours. I feel keenly and sorrowfully the latter-day identification of the Jewish community with some of the more illiberal elements in American society. Not to remark on that circumstance would lend my comments about blacks and Jews and matters of justice no sense at all.

I feel that my observations about black judges are much more harsh than anything I have said about judges from other ethnic or racial groups. Certainly, it is not my intention to spread hate by my specific references. It is that I believe that Jews have suffered so many of the same kinds of slings and arrows as those endured by blacks that those in a position to do so should do more. If blacks remain isolated from their natural Jewish allies, I believe that both will be at the mercy of an irremedial peril.

Horace Walpole, the fourth Earl of Orford, remarked more than two hundred years ago that "This world is a comedy to those that think, a tragedy to those that feel." It becomes a bit more complex for those who both think and feel and who cannot escape either burden.

Does the cumulative impact of the vignettes I shall describe make for melancholia? Nevertheless, I cherish the law as a source of America's possibilities, its rehabilitation and healing from the wounds of slavery and its social and legal consequences.

One day, perhaps, those of us who wear the black robe will have a university that will prepare us for that great calling to the bench. We may then cherish a hope to live up to the highest and most humane of our loftiest slogans.

Cut into the stone pillars outside New York City's Criminal Courts Building are hopeful legends: "Equal and exact justice to all men of whatever state or persuasion." These words of Thomas Jefferson greet those entering the oldest court of general sessions in America. Just beyond that hopeful phrase, one is further encouraged to believe that alert and zealous guardians sit, tender of mercy and fierce in their guarantee that the law must never stray into error. ". . . where law ends, tyranny begins." Thus had William Pitt concluded a speech on England's constitution in 1770. It is ironic that Jefferson was a slaveowner and Pitt an abolitionist. An American parallel, coming much later, is found in the epic sculptures cut into the Black Hills of North Dakota. There, Gutzon Borglum included both Washington and Lincoln. One was a slaveowner; the other is known as the Great Emancipator.

In such things, large and small, do we see the confused patterns of American life. "There is nothing wrong with Americans," said G. K. Chesterton, "except their ideals." Perhaps they, as is the case with some of us who judge, need the rehabilitation our law so much neglects in those we condemn.

New York City
1987

Black Robes, White Justice

1

The Influence of the Early Years

White people are conditioned from the time of their birth to the preferred status of their skin color. Their views of the world at large and their own environment become solidified by circumstances, presuppositions, myths, clichés, and traditional folklore. Too many have a reaction to color prejudice that parallels that of Franklin D. Roosevelt in 1941. During World War II, he could always excuse his inattention to the so-called "Negro Problem" by saying that, for national security, he was compelled to concentrate on the Allied mission to win the war.

It was evident, nevertheless, that Roosevelt preferred racial matters just the way they then were in America. The racial segregation of public facilities in Washington, D.C., was presided over by F.D.R. just as he had found it when he arrived there. It was not to be changed by him. When Conrad Lynn sued to enjoin the induction of his brother into the Army, he claimed that racial segregation in the armed forces was unconstitutional. When asked to comment on a unique and disturbing focus on a flaw in democracy, Roosevelt asked, "What's wrong with it? We've always done that."

In 1897, such reasoning was found "revolting" by Oliver Wendell Holmes. He wrote about how pathetic it is "to have no better reason for a rule of law than that so it was laid down in the time of Henry IV," whose reign in England spanned the years between 1399 and 1413.[1]

As conservatives, the white population accepted society as they found it. Most Americans have never been agitators for change in a philosophical sense. Those who did agitate were few and regarded at best by the majority as quixotic, odd, different, not quite normal. Worse yet, they may have been suspected of being Communists.

It is from the most conservative segment of a well-behaved society that our judges are chosen. Those who are regarded as radicals seldom manage either appointment or election to the bench. Indeed, radicals are a suspect segment of society. They are more associated with the destruction of government than with building and running it. With most Americans, the term "radical" is inseparable from that badge of infamy which classified one as a red, a syndicalist or a Bolshevik.

National head-shaking was occasioned by the numbers of white and respectable children turning to Students for a Democratic Society or the Weathermen, or making some sympathetic identification with the Black Panthers. There was utter consternation when Patricia Hearst was revealed as an armed member of the Symbionese Liberation Army and its escapades, which were not only rebellious but criminal.

While there were young lawyers anxious to defend radicals, seldom if ever were lawyers to be found among the ranks of the rebels themselves. One certainly never hears of lawyers for such groups being elevated to the bench. Lawyers, anxious to alter

the direction of society or urge reforms proceed with musty caution. They are patient, careful, and reliant upon what they like
to call the democratic process.

Judges themselves, when on the brink of a decision that will
change some aspect of life, or be different from ancient precedent, are always careful to hedge their opinions with moralizing.
The law, it is believed, should reach no social goal unless the
governing power of a community has made up its mind that that
is what it wants. This was stated as an 1899 view of Holmes and
it remains so to this day. And yet, there are times when the law
appears to be radical, or at least progressive; when it does things
by fiat which it believes the legislative bodies should have done
by statute.

Black radicals, of course, have no patience with such a complicated and uncertain process. They *know* what most communities
have made up their minds about and what is thought of them.
These blacks have written off white society as impossible to
change in its attitude toward color. Some call themselves Five
Percenters. All the other blacks, they say, are Uncle Toms, making subservient obeisance to the system. For them, burglary,
robbery, and worse have become the legitimate purpose of survival. They are wrong, of course, but they do not care to know
that. Some whisper that anything they can get away with is
justified.

They are not radicals. It may well be that there are no black
radicals in modern society. Nat Turner's murders and bloody
reach for freedom from slavery were the elements of radical conduct. The destruction of a slaveowner destroyed slaveowning for
that master, at least. It served as a warning to others that the
"peculiar institution" was not quite in accord with the people of
the United States securing the blessings of justice and liberty,
either to themselves or their posterity.

Some blacks, waging intellectual guerilla warfare, have suggested that the Washington and Jefferson Monuments should be

bombed to ashes as a latter-day expression of black resentment against slavery. But even the most charismatic, angry and emotional advocates of black power have always insisted upon their Constitutional rights when captured.

White radicals often win that pejorative title simply by identifying with some unpopular cause or by identifying their own ideals for a nation's propriety with those of blacks, Indians or Hispanic Americans. The conduct of white radicals has often been directed against what is regarded as a suspect national purpose.

For a time, during the war in Vietnam, draft resisters fled to Canada or sought asylum elsewhere. Some burned their draft cards and went to prison. Some Roman Catholic priests who acted out their faith in the natural law poured blood on draft records. The 1968 Democratic National Convention was the target of other young whites who expressed their angry impatience with the country's sense of direction. Nevertheless it would be difficult for white radicals to understand the pathos and, all too often, the doom of the black struggle. While the white radicals have passed through various and periodic causes, often as though dictated by fashion, the black ordeal for creating a basis for radical conduct has been a continuing one for over three hundred years in America.

It is the *déjà vu* quality of the struggle which has discouraged so many blacks. Opposition to repression has hit highs and lows. Frederick Douglass's sense of the enormity of the white-black friction in America compelled him to remind posterity, through his last will and testament, never to forget the urgent necessity to agitate, agitate, agitate. Opposition to racism by blacks, then, is not a matter of fashion; it is a matter of survival.

Where many blacks disagree is in the techniques of opposition. The blacks who believe they have it made, and who feel secure in their token roles in the establishment, do not regard themselves as tokens. They are well behaved and well rewarded. They might participate in the kind of march on Washington that is a non-violent picnic to which they actually fly, or go by train or chartered bus. On the other hand, they would never dream of picketing a business for its failure to hire blacks, Hispanics, Jews or women. Nor would they be caught carrying a sign with a screaming slogan. Black lawyers who emerge from such non-involved and well-behaved groups to become judges may be expected to be little different from the most ordinary white judge, and to identify closely with the very establishment which so-called black radicals oppose.

Except for the capitalist rebels of 1776, who disliked the business of King George III, America has been free of those revolutions and *coups* that place left-wing extremists in the power places of government. In America, there has never been an example of the oppressed, when liberated, becoming the oppressor.

It is the rare and unusual white person who will revolt, even within the limits of Constitutional speech and public declarations, against this country's way of life. After all, his color allows him to be a beneficiary of that way of life. It is an even more unusual white who can consider his fellow man just another person, as opposed to a "colored" person, a "Negro friend," or a "black" one. The use of such terms to refer to another human being imposes an immediate classification. It is an indication that a "colored person" is not simply another citizen, but something less. The description is an instruction to the listener of *how* such a person of color must be regarded, not only as different, but as diminished in status as well. It is a debased and debasing classification.

There have been genuine relationships of affection and mutual esteem between whites and blacks, and I am willing to believe that each could regard the other simply as a human being and not as "my black friend" or my "white friend." All too often, white humanitarians decline in their zeal for equality, move to the white suburbs, and become occasional liberals with black visitors now and then.

***

Racism inside the courts is but a reflection of what goes on in society in general. This was brought home forcefully to me with a kind of grim humor in 1974. At that time I was teaching a course at The New School for Social Research in the evenings, as well as an early morning one at Staten Island Community College. This called for some tense traveling in order not to be late in reporting to court. After leaving Staten Island, I would speed across the Verrazano Bridge to be in my courtroom by 10 A.M.

One afternoon, during a trial, I felt so faint and weak I could not carry on. The clerks, with affectionate concern, feared that I was having a heart attack. I was taken out of the courthouse lashed to a stretcher. It was an embarrassment to be so helpless and publicly exhibited.

In the emergency room of the hospital, I was placed in a curtained-off area where there were two beds some distance apart. On one was a white man, obviously one of the poor derelicts now and then brought in from the Bowery. He appeared to be in a state of joyous alcoholic bewilderment. He needed a shave; neither his soiled sneakers nor his socks matched; he drooled a bit and sang softly in garbled syllables.

As I watched him from my bed, I felt pangs of pity. He seemed much worse off than I. I felt guilty for being dressed in a three-piece suit and clean shirt.

I heard a nurse outside the curtained area say, "Hurry, doctor, we have a judge who is ill." A white doctor parted the curtains, paused at the entrance, looked at me and then at the white derelict. He hurried to the side of the white man, lifted his wrist, as though to test his pulse, and said, "Judge, what seems to be the matter?"

It was a bracing experience, wholly therapeutic, and I began to recover without delay.

The most remarkable aspect of the hospital experience was the reinforcement of my view that whites almost automatically have a "place" reaction to the color of dark skin. Compared with a poor, ragged, homeless white unfortunate, unshaven and drooling, a well-dressed black simply could not be the judge. What a sadness, I thought, and how appropriate was the observation of an unknown wit who had said that America was the only country in the world to suffer a decline and fall in its civilization without first becoming civilized.

I had some time before perceived American reaction to color to be synonymous with a conspiracy to de-develop the black *persona* and keep blacks so busy defending their right to exist that all of their energies would be diverted and they would thus retrogress, becoming, officially, the American untouchables, its aboriginals, caught in a static posture of non-evolving. We were not even supposed to reach the status of that exceptional African whom the French colonial masters so contemptuously referred to as the *évolué*."

***

Because of some of the more publicized decisions I have made from the bench, the mail that I continue to receive is, for the most part, unprintable in its scatological filth and references to incestuous sexual perversion. Its constant theme, however, is, "Nigger judge, go back to Africa and learn from the apes."

One author of bitter racist literature has apparently discovered the secret of both life and death. He never fails to urge me to "Drop dead. Drop dead twice." A Christmas present, repeated each year since 1972, is unfailingly delivered to the

courthouse for me. It is in an elaborately and beautifully
wrapped Tiffany box, complete with a professionally tied ribbon.
Inside, there is always a quantity of human feces.

A cliché in the law is that it must change as the views of people change. Thus, progress can be marked by the whole truths of
one generation becoming the half-truths or even the non-truths
of the next. It is in that way that ancient folkways and
mythologies are altered and society escapes its old but only
sometimes useless ruts.

The emotionalism generated by the sight of dark skin seems
wholly to annul all possibility of intellectual progress. It is this
eternal vision of pigmentation that appears to control American
racial conduct. Naturally, most whites among whom the subject
is raised deny vehemently that demons of color bias trouble the
purity of their reasoning.

At a weekend meeting of judges sponsored by federal funds
and luxuriously housed at a converted baronial estate on Long
Island, I was the black member of a panel analyzing problems of
the judiciary. A question was posed, as I later learned, to bait
remarks from me. The question was, "Would you treat the following two defendants differently? A well-dressed and well-
educated white man stands before the bar, accused of having
stolen a pair of trousers from Macy's department store. The
price tag was $30.00, the size was 36 and the color was blue. A
black man, obviously uneducated from his manner of speech,
and probably illiterate, also stands accused of having stolen a
pair of trousers from Macy's. They, too, had a price tag of
$30.00, were size 36 and were blue. The black defendant is
dressed in filthy rags and sports a disheveled Afro hairdo. He
looks fairly ferocious."

One by one, the priests of justice answered with anxious nays
that, under no circumstances, would they give different treatment to the two contrasting defendants, and they uttered sol-

26

emn assurances that both would be treated with evenhanded objectivity. After all, the underlying theme went, shoplifting is shoplifting, no matter who does it. Quite clearly, however, from the word picture presented to the panel, the white defendant did not *need* to shoplift, while the black example appeared to be in need of clothing.

My interruption of so many paeans of self-praise and instant objectivity was a lost effort to satirize their pomp. I said that I did not believe any of them and that, confronted with such a melancholy spectacle, they would react as society had trained them to react; that somehow, the skin color of the black defendant would have effect upon what they would do; and that the black defendant would probably be dealt with differently and more harshly than the white *because* he was black.

The unison of ire aroused by that accusation was an instant revival of the ancient Greek chorus. Ignoring the Kenneth Tynan description of a satirist as a "demolition expert" who never fills the vacuum he creates, I said that, since the white defendant resembled most of the judges themselves, they would feel bound to justify various aspects of Pascal's theory of self-sympathy. From the decibels of denial and head shaking, the voice of one judge emerged. In my early days on the bench, he had been extremely kind to me and had, in fact, on a hot and stuffy day of numerous arraignments, voluntarily offered invaluable assistance.

He said, "Bruce, your trouble is that you're hung up on the question of race. Everything is race with you. We never see the color of a defendant's skin when he stands before the bench. Just the other day, I had a little colored kid before me. . ."

His voice trailed off, as though he had suddenly realized his tumble from the fragile perch of uncontaminated reason. But could he understand the beneficial discrimination that might flow from sorrow, and the emotion induced by such a pathetic sight as the black and ragged defendant?

***

The hard fact is that none of us knows what to do about crime, other than hope that our persons and our homes will be secure. In our desperation to do something, we send offenders to jail. There is no other place to send them. Judges, divorced from the way of life of the streets, hear a catalogue of crimes read off and charged to a defendant. They are appalled. They are shocked. They become angry. They realize that they are really a security force and keepers of the peace. In their minds, they convict the defendant. He is the menace, a danger to society.

The judge believes that there really *is* a criminal class, whose mission is to prey upon both the wary and the unwary. Their language is different from that of the judicial class. They mumble out their pleas. They put on the false faces of humility or defiance. Their very postures dissemble. They are embarrassed not because of their public exposure, but because they've failed in their craft and been caught.

As with politicians trapped on videotape, it is the failure to defeat detection which is the ultimate offense against themselves. Somehow, those of us who sit in judgment suspect that the defendants are plotting to do better when they get out—that is, better at avoiding the respectable traps laid for them by society.

***

Built into society is a natural kind of racist animus. There is always a tendency to support, protect, and preserve a system in which one has a preferred role. Most of the judges of America are white. They value the system that has elevated them to such prominence within it. Criminals are the enemies of such a system. Criminals, in fact, are the justification for the existence of a judicial system. Judges, then, may be expected to have a high regard for themselves and their way of life.

An inward turning permits judicial narcissism to become a mirror, reflecting both the judges' class comfort and the menace presented by crime and those who commit it. If the system is to survive, the offenders must be disposed of. Prisons and the death penalty, thus far, appear to be the only answer, despite their failure.

To plan long-term responses to crime and criminal behavior is obviously too burdensome for a society that has found comfort in quick answers, quick-food, Polaroid pictures, and other immediate-result inventions. It is as though we have said to ourselves, "If it cannot be done immediately, then perhaps fate does not want it done and it should not be done."

I'm convinced that so long as Americans can see the darkness of skin color, just so long will they feel that discrimination based on that perception is natural and moral. That implanted view, which is inseparable from American history and the national preference for white skin, presents a problem that may be insoluble.

Clearly, no solutions are offered by our present system of racial exclusion from so many of the blessings and benefits of society. For some of us, theories of justice will occupy our sense of inquiry forever, hoping for the discovery, accidental or otherwise, of a solution to the disease-like irritation of crime, which will promote justice as fairness, and from which the taint of racism will be absent.

To be the product of a white mother and a black father is fairly meaningless until it is brought forcefully to a child's attention. The distinction between two colors is always there, of course. But for the child the real meaning of color in America is not. Heedless of ancient folkways and compelled beliefs, a child simply has a mother and a father. Living in a black neighborhood as we did, certifies the normalcy of people of different colors. Of course, the experts say that by the time a black child is three, he recognizes the different shades of skin color. But the recognition of the sociology of different colors comes later, and then only gradually. In the end it becomes an emotional avalanche.

My earliest recalled experiences of feeling that a dark skin made a negative difference to those with white skins occurred when I was about six or seven. My maternal grandparents celebrated their fiftieth wedding anniversary in an armory. They had thirteen children and all of those children had offspring. With all the in-laws and friends, an armory was necessary. One boy, about my age, asked me if I was a nigger. He asked me in such a way that I immediately said no. The word was not new to me, but I had never thought of myself in such terms. That was the beginning, the first rumble of impending turmoil.

The next rumble, louder this time, came the following spring, or perhaps the one after that. I was allowed to walk alone on the beach in Rockaway, a big treat for a little boy, while my Aunt Catherine sat in her Oldsmobile and watched.

Several white youths approached. One said, "No niggers are allowed here," and he and his friends rushed toward me. I ran as fast as I could back to my aunt's car, where the boys confronted her and asked her why she was protecting "that nigger." She made no reply to their insults, but the awareness of difference continued its inexorable growth.

Later that year I was in a grocery store with my mother. Thanksgiving was approaching. One of the employees pointed to a basket of nuts and said, "These are some of the best 'nigger-toes' we've had in a long time." My mother said nothing, and we walked out of the store.

None of these experiences, however, transformed me into an angry rebel. After all, I was taking violin lessons from a white teacher. Most of my school teachers were white. My two closest friends were Prosper Cima and Tony Ferrara who, if they thought about it, never mentioned race. In the ninth grade, I shared first prize in a poster contest with a white girl. Our prize was two tickets to Sheridan's *The School for Scandal*. We sat next to each other in the theater and she asked that I see her safely home.

Inevitably—I wonder if it is so for all blacks—there was a period when I passionately wanted to be white, or at least be like whites. The violin lessons helped nourish that sad dream. When a fellow member of the high school hockey team told me with great enthusiasm after a game, "If you had a bag over your head, we wouldn't even know you were colored," instead of being insulted, I felt I was succeeding in my masquerade. Although I always believed I was extremely sensitive, the implications of that remark were lost in my secret joy.

Of course, I avoided watermelon and took only academic studies—no shop classes for Bruce Wright, no sir!—as though I were preparing my parents to send me to an Ivy League university in the midst of the Great Depression. Since the major Olympic stars of the time were Jesse Owens and Ralph Metcalf, I naturally elected to avoid the sprints and I became a tortured miler and cross-country runner.

I was the black goal tender on the soccer team. I was there to protect my white allies, a Horatius at the bridge over the Tiber. Had that dream been a part of the false faces of the televised seventies and eighties instead of the thirties, after each game my teammates and I would have shared a joyous beer with my smiling presence integrating the scene.

My sister and brother seemed impervious to the kinds of confusions that harassed my childhood. My brother grew to be over six feet tall with a splendid physique. Fair of skin and with legs that resembled those of a Greek statue, he was always quiet and conservative. He was never known to curse and he seemed to identify closely with our grandfather. Introspective and practical, he made things with his hands and loved the quiet inactivity of fishing. He thought about things for a long time before acting and I never knew him to yield to an impulse. I was not surprised when, after nearly thirty years of marriage, I learned that he was getting a divorce. When I asked him what happened, he merely said, "I've been thinking about it for twenty-five years."

Many of his friends were white and all of his business associates were. After World War II, he said that the thing he wanted most was to have a mink farm. With his army savings, he bought some remote acreage in New Jersey near New Brunswick and established his farm. This called for travels as distant as Canada for that business and he was away for extended periods of time.

I never understood this allegiance to New Jersey. We had been born there, he in Newark and my sister and I in Princeton. My earliest days—those before school began—were spent in Ossining, New York, and after I went off to college I spent virtually no time in Princeton. But my life was lashed to that place by one circumstance or another. The beauty of its pre-revolutionary scenes was marred by its curious racism, a quiet virulence that both whites and blacks accepted as normal and unremarkable.

One of my teachers there, Caroline P. Gates, was black. She would have been regarded as a radical had her historical views been widely known in that solidly Republican village. She expressed delight about my violin lessons and my anxiety to read everything. She introduced me to the writings of people I had never heard about—Harriet Tubman, Sojourner Truth, Phyllis Wheatley, Nat Turner, Denmark Vesey and the black crew of the *Amistad* that had rebelled against slave traders and taken over the ship. After school on non-violin-lesson days, she would tell me of the Underground Railroad and of the hypocrisy of George Washington and Thomas Jefferson as slaveowners.

It was from Caroline Gates that I heard of Paul Robeson and how Princeton had rejected that heroic giant. I had known nothing of that when I sat in my father's lap and heard Robeson in concert in Witherspoon Hall on the Princeton campus.

Little did I dream that one day Princeton would give me the same distinction of rejection it had given Robeson. That quiet little Central Jersey academic retreat was a bitter paradox. Its university boasted of service to the world and pointed with pride to Woodrow Wilson, a Southerner who had taught Constitutional Law. His first executive order after becoming President was to segregate Washington's public facilities. After that, and until the sixties, those facilities were no longer public, only white.

Princeton was compared by Robeson with a "Georgia plantation town," and it fully justified that comparison. It was because of that famous citadel of learning, that refuge for Einstein and Thomas Mann and other persecuted intellectuals, that I was to turn my back on Christianity and ridicule its pretensions, its pomp and rituals, especially as exhibited in the half-royal, half-pagan trappings of Roman Catholicism, the branch of Christianity into which I had been born.

It was the Christians who ran Princeton University, who had a quota for Jews, who rejected Negroes completely. It was indeed a curious place. The town, dominated by the university, differed in no large degree from that institution. Blacks were huddled behind Princeton's main street, and their enclave continued on down to the unpaved "avenues" next to the trolley tracks that ran to Trenton, past the adjacent dump. Oddly, Italians, too, lived in the heart of the Negro neighborhood and some of their children became my closest friends.

The Y.M.C.A., as though on a civilizing mission to a primitive people, had established itself on Witherspoon Street, converting a vacant residential building to black use. A yard became an ill-kept tennis court. A pool table provided diversion in one room and in another there was a ping-pong table. Presiding over this racial oasis was one John Redmond, whose Indian forebears had left their mark upon him. He said he slept with a pistol under his pillow as a tribute to the racism of Princeton.

With a black Y.M.C.A. and none for the whites, elements of that popular myth, reverse discrimination, might be discerned.

33

However, the "Y.M.C.A." was part of the University itself. Whites and whites only were allowed to use Princeton's gymnasium, swimming pool, tennis courts and playing fields. Blacks were excluded, totally and without exception.

When I was fourteen and the black member of my high school's hockey team, our schedule called for a game with Princeton's freshmen. The coach, George Tindall, was fond of emphasizing his Scottish heritage. He also emphasized his amazement that I was able to make the team.

The team arrived at the entrance of the Hobey Baker Memorial Rink on the campus and I was stopped at the doorway and not allowed to enter. "No coloreds are allowed in here," said a voice, branding my brain. Tindall said nothing. He gave me a quick glance and ushered in the other team members.

I suppose that I expected something more of him. Tears and fury mixed as I turned away. I was never able thereafter to speak to any of the team members or to Tindall. The experience stunned me for a long time. Later I would have another Princeton incident.

The days of my youth were the years of the Depression, and the poverty of the time was obvious everywhere in Princeton, except at the university. It was generally believed that the college was a luxurious and private reservation for the rich—rich males. In those days women, like Negroes, were not tolerated, either as professors or students.

During the winter and spring months, the town dump was a particularly busy place, as black boys and girls could be seen sifting through ashes piled there picking out unburned coal to take home. The universality of America's crisis was brought home to me by travels with my Aunt Catherine. Along Riverside Park in New York there were the tents and lean-tos of those who were otherwise homeless. Blacks in Princeton were somewhat luckier in their modest comforts. The rich students needed waiters and porters for their exclusive residential clubs, the University's substitute for fraternities. Professors, and executives who commuted to New York each day, needed domestics. The black labor supply filled these jobs.

Negroes also worked in the kitchens and dining halls of the university. A black man ran a one-car taxi fleet based in front of the university. His clientele was white only, and he was always in demand.

The most successful black entrepreneur was a man named Griggs, who had a restaurant where some of the university teams maintained training tables. In the Negro neighborhood, there was only one black business, a combination grocery store and butcher shop. Another resident was a contractor who had built the loveliest home in the ghetto. Everyone assumed he was wealthy.

Two public elementary schools served the area. The Witherspoon School was all black, with both black and white teachers. The other was known as the Township School. It was all white, as were its teachers. The general population of the black community assumed it was a private school although it was not. All of the whites who lived in the Negro area attended either that school or the Catholic school on Nassau Street. There, out of deference to the Society for the Propagation of the Faith and Proselytizing, a handful of black Catholics was allowed to attend.

Strangely, the high school student body was integrated, although the teaching staff was not. Presumably it would have been too expensive, even for spurious separate-but-equal desires, to have two high schools. In any event, not many black students got that far or endured, once there. It was a reflection of the hopelessness of the times, I suppose.

There were few professional role models for black children. Black university graduates worked as waiters, or in the post office, or were unemployed. The two children of the taxi driver had gone off to a black college in Virginia. One returned after graduation to take over his father's business—all that education in order to drive a cab. . . . The daughter became a teacher in the all-black school of her student days.

Most of those who went beyond high school came back to the town, except for one who remained at his black college as a coach. Perhaps the others saw the future integration of the place and were patient enough to wait. I had neither religion nor hope to keep me there. Aunt Catherine was my Underground Railroad. Travels in her various Oldsmobiles were an exciting education without books.

My education would embrace many insights into my fellow blacks, insights that would not endear me to them or them to me. They were blacks who had never been in trouble and who would never be in typical American racist trouble. It might be better said that they would never realize the trouble symbolized by their visible race.

Despite what should have been the reality of my perceptions, I had thought that I would attend Princeton University. A scholarship arranged for me by one of my high school instructors had brought joy to a family that had no money. We were, after all, in the midst of the Great Depression.

I stood in the registration line full of hope. The sun was shining and the green lawns of the University were beautiful to behold. In my innocence I was untroubled when an upperclassman, an orange arm-band identifying his status, asked me to follow him to the office of the director of admissions.

I was ushered into the presence of Radcliffe Heermance. This man of Falstaffian girth towered over me. Light shafted through the leaded windows of the office. Heermance stood there, as though surrounded by a divine radiance. He was the first man to address me as "Mr. Wright." His next words, however, would destroy much of the child and educate me beyond anything I would ever learn in a classroom.

"We did not know you were colored when the scholarship was arranged."

I do not remember if his face was kindly as he uttered those words. They reminded me of the night, only months before, when I had graduated from high school. I had wandered idly from one block to another, full of apprehension about an uncertain future in a time of national poverty. As I walked, I noticed a white man sitting with his chair tilted back against the wall of a bar, listening intently to a radio playing within. Suddenly the man leaped to his feet, virtually in front of me. He slammed one fist violently into his other hand and yelled, "At last, they got that black son-of-a-bitch!" I later learned that Max Schmeling had just knocked out Joe Louis in their first fight. From that experience and from others that had preceded it, it would seem that racism should have used up most of its rude surprises for me.

Yet there were to be many more. One came closely behind the Princeton slap. For many on my mother's side of the family, the Pope was president of the world's only true faith. His claim of infallibility was matched by the perfection of my mother's trust in patron saints, miraculous medals, and the joy of prayer.

The answer to Princeton's Protestant antipathy was obviously Roman Catholic piety and propriety. Notre Dame, the most famous of the Catholic universities, would surely welcome my coming. An application there was made to sound within the family like a religious event. As it developed, however, the only difference between Princeton and Notre Dame was one of physical distance—and perhaps a more courteous rejection. A letter over the signature of a priest included certain historical references that made it an apologia. I was informed that Notre Dame's first president had been a slave-owner, but that he had freed his slaves before coming to South Bend, Indiana, to head the University.

Lincoln University, where I was finally admitted, was the first college in America to have been founded to educate blacks. Slavery was still the law of the land when it opened its doors in 1854. Its fertile countryside in rural Chester County, Pennsylvania, was known to harbor sympathies for the Ku Klux Klan. Most of the professors were white.

Lincoln University was the alma mater of Nnamdi Azikiwe, the first leader of liberated Nigeria, and of Kwame Nkrumah, who led the Gold Coast to independence from Britain and to a return to its ancient name, Ghana.

The nearest town to the University was Oxford, a racially segregated village, where one could be diverted at its movie house if willing to sit in the balcony, where all Negroes were sent. There was little difference between life in that tiny place and south of the Mason-Dixon Line, which was not far away.

In 1941, during my junior year at Lincoln, I was a passenger in a car that spun out of control at a curve on the edge of Oxford and turned over. A classmate, thrown through the roof of the car, lay on the shoulder of the road with a fractured and bleeding skull. Unconscious, his head lay in my lap. We remained there for over three hours. The local hospital would not admit Negroes and no doctor would come to the roadside. We waited, all five of us, until an ambulance from the University of Pennsylvania Hospital arrived from Philadelphia, sixty miles away.

I mention these things by way of showing that I should not have been terribly surprised by manifestations of racism in the American justice system. I've often wondered why I was so naive about my own experience with it. I must have suffered from, and with, the usual American dreams of a first-generation son of an immigrant.

My non-professional father's preoccupation with the professions centered only on me and on my becoming a doctor. He hoped that going to college would be the irresistible first step toward medical school. But Lincoln University's laboratory courses for pre-medical students used live rabbits and stray cats.

They were anesthetized and students were expected to master elementary uses of the scalpel on living flesh. A born coward and committed pacifist, I could not bear the sight of blood without feeling the pain of the knife's intrusion—and becoming nauseous.

Although my father's ambitions were temporarily dashed, I felt the release from this paternal burden when I decided that what I really wanted was to become a lawyer.

Franklin H. Williams, a year ahead of me in college, was headed for law school, and I was awe-struck by his ability to make public addresses. He had become one of my heroes, and I was obsessed by the naive idea that, as a lawyer, I would be better able to aid and abet the survival of Negroes. The law was a vast storehouse of exotic secrets. And so I applied to Fordham University.

In law school, often as the only black in my class, first at Fordham and later at New York Law School, I marveled at the apparent ease of white students discussing commercial cases in class. It took a great deal of self-conscious effort to remember that I wanted to be like Frank Williams. It was no help to my confidence when a white female student sat down next to me in the library one day and said, with seeming sincerity, "You know, Bruce, if you weren't colored, I'd like for you to take me to the class prom." All I could mutter was, "I'd love to take you, if you weren't white." Neither of us apparently knew at the time that Essex House where the prom was scheduled, had told the class secretary not to have any Negroes present.

The entire law school experience was something of a failure from my idealistic perspective. If I were to be a legal savior for the black race, it seemed to me that there was a vast area of the law I would have to study which was being wholly ignored by my school. Racial restrictive covenants, for example, which served to imprison blacks in ghetto neighborhoods, promised some intellectual heat and excitement. However, my professor

39

said, in a terse dismissal of their importance as a subject, "All you need to know is that the courts generally uphold such covenants." Similarly, voting rights cases were given no analysis. In criminal law, there was no discussion of the famous Scottsboro case, which had had such a bitter effect on black minds throughout the country. This was either intellectual or emotional racism, or perhaps a mixture of both.

The more I researched such cases on my own, the angrier I became with American society and the more I wondered how Supreme Court justices could be referred to as great jurists. Oliver Wendell Holmes and Benjamin N. Cardozo became tarnished giants of the law. It seemed so simple to me for them to have voted enthusiastically for the same Constitutional rights for blacks as those they supported for whites. Instead, I found some of their opinions to be lost in philosophical technicalities, as though a citizen's color was an officially disqualifying disease. Suddenly, law school became a self-help discipline, a bifurcated intermediate career.

On one hand, I had the white studies of the regular curriculum; on the other, the private melancholia of reading the civil rights cases. It was then, as I regarded my white fellow-students, that I decided they could never really be my friends unless they came to feel, and expressed, some of the same outrage that had come over me. That this was an impossible condition to impose for friendship, I knew. Nevertheless, to this day, I have refused to attend reunions of my law school class. There are distances that can never be bridged.

I know, now, that I wanted them to take sides, never realizing that they had already done so, although not "my" side. And they never would. It was as simple as William Faulkner made it appear when interviewed by *Life* magazine after winning his Nobel prize. He said that of course the black struggle was justified, but if it came to combat in the streets between blacks and whites, he would be on the side of the whites.

40

2

Random Thoughts from a Life Long Lived

When in February, 1970, I began my untranquil tenure as a Criminal Court judge, it was not a career I could have anticipated or prepared for. There was nothing in my life that remotely suggested that I would ever have an active role in politics, nor did I ever have any ambition to be a judge. I was fifty years of age, a bit late to be coming to the bench, although not an unusual age for the few blacks who did manage to become judges. I had always been an adversary of the system, as opposed to one of its functionaries. I had some fairly heavy baggage of remembered experiences, including service in the United States Army during World War II. One of my mistakes was seeking to match logic against military attitudes and the impatience of the military mind with reason.

41

Sent from New York to Camp Rucker, Alabama, I could not understand racial segregation in a democratic army that was fighting against Nazi and fascist racism. One experience in Alabama that resulted in a court martial and punishment that could have been worse, was a harsh lesson. Most of the black troops at Camp Rucker were in a quartermaster or service battalion. When a white artillery unit managed to set local woods on fire with its practice shots, the black unit was called out to fight the fire.

I requested permission to see the company captain, as I had a right to do. We had had confrontations before. He demanded to know my business. I told him that under no circumstances could I help put out the fire. Livid, he asked if I was crazy. I told him that countless Negroes had been lynched on trees in Alabama and that I hoped that all of the state's trees would burn down and perhaps spread to neighboring Confederate states. The captain, showing no patience for my knowledge of neighboring geography, yelled to the company's first sergeant to take me away. Accused of insubordination, I eventually stood trial. My socio-historical arguments were brushed aside. Many of us referred to the camp as Camp Mother Rucker.

My experiences in Alabama had not prospered from my first day there. I had arrived with several other university students and graduates, including my track coach at Lincoln University. We were greeted by a Captain Hopke, an officer from Sikeston, Missouri, where a Negro man had been lynched in a particularly barbaric fashion. He asked each of us to recite names, rank and serial numbers, just as they appeared on our service records. When the captain reached me, I said, "Bruce McM. Wright, private, parenthesis Colored, close parenthesis." He was furious and said he was not going to have any smart-ass sons of bitches in his outfit. Worse was to come.

Camp Rucker was in a dry county of the state and each weekend soldiers with passes would rush off to Panama City, Florida, where alcohol was not prohibited. Before being dismissed for the weekend, however, there was always inspection of the troops conducted by a major. One Saturday, as the company stood at attention, the major swaggered before us and said, "I thought I told you boys to make your mess kits shine like a nigger's heel." My immediate dialogue with him resulted in extra duty and triggered furious efforts to be in touch with congressmen from New York and somehow get a transfer to the segregated Air Force then training in Tuskegee Institute in another part of Alabama. Much later I learned that none of my letters ever left Camp Rucker.

Finally sent overseas, first to Scotland, then to Liverpool and thereafter to Wales, I was assigned to a medical detachment where I remained until Dwight D. Eisenhower addressed a message to "The Negro Troops." With more casualties than he had anticipated in the North African campaign, the general said that we might then volunteer for the combat infantry, where our "white brothers" had borne the brunt, as though we had been slackers. I was a coward, certainly, but not a slacker. I volunteered, along with a few thousand others. Overwhelmed by the response, those in charge imposed new intellectual and physical standards to weed out some, and, ultimately, about three thousand were accepted to be distributed among selected infantry divisions.

Assigned to the First Infantry Division's 26th Regiment, with a few other blacks, I arrived at my company and we were greeted by a short, angry captain. His welcome was memorable: "I never thought I'd live to see the day when a nigger would wear the Big Red One." It was Alabama transported across the seas. The black presence in the division may have changed in the surface way of our presence but not in white fundamental attitudes.

When I was wounded in France, healed and ready to rejoin my company, a white sergeant called out the names of all of the other soldiers gathered near two trucks.

"Listen up for your names," he said. "If you're white, stand over here; if you're colored, stand over there."

And yet, all of us were going to the same division.

When the war was over, the process of racial conditioning continued. Selected to be returned to the United States because of the points I had accumulated by reason of time overseas, I walked onto a naval vessel with others. I carried my duffel bag of souvenirs and a typewriter I had looted in Czechoslovakia and wore all of my medals and decorations, including a combat infantryman's badge. A naval officer, staring at me, said to a fellow officer, "I didn't know niggers were fighting." A few steps along, I did a right-about-face and walked off the ship. I took a third-class car on a train bound for Paris, where I remained until caught and shipped back to the States.

In Paris, I looked up Leopold Sedar Senghor, then a classics professor in the Colonial University. The first sub-Saharan African to win a Ph.D. degree in France, he was very much a black Frenchman. He and I had met shortly after the liberation of Paris while my unit was on an eight-hour pass. I was introduced to him as a black American poet. Some of my poems had been published in Cardiff after D-Day and while I was then across the Channel. A former classmate at Lincoln had somewhat excessively described me as a published poet.

Senghor, of course, was widely known as a great intellectual and poet. He later became a senator for Senegal and, after the independence of Senegal, he became the country's President. He looked after me and fed me during my stay in Paris. Eventually, he assigned Professor Louis Achille, of Lyon, to translate my poetry and to prepare it for a bilingual edition. The project never occurred and it was only after my return to New York that

Langston Hughes and I became friends, and he did much to help me publish some of my poetry in various quarterlies.

Back in New York, I completed my law school studies and became an associate in the firm of Proskauer Rose Goetz & Mendelsohn, where there had never been a black associate. The Proskauer firm is more than one hundred years old and enjoyed, as it does now, great prestige. It is what is known as a Jewish firm and is doubtless a product of those not-so-distant days when discrimination among the Christian firms barred Jews from membership there. My experience there introduced me to a well-dressed world of carefully preened young intellectuals and starched respectability. Its corporate clients were light-years distant from the plebeian harshness of crime.

I was in the midst of exciting new experiences and learning from the inside things that had only been touched upon in law school. As the first black lawyer in that firm, I was, of course, a token. I formed lasting relationships with Edward Silver, Harold Levin and Philip Haberman, Jr. All three did much to aid my career.

Silver risked his own career in the firm by nominating me for a partnership in 1968. I had left the firm long before that, when the managing partner, Bernard Lang, told me that I could stay as long as I wished, but that I would never become a partner. The firm's clients, he said, were not ready for a Negro partner. That was 1951.

The year 1968, Silver said, was different, but it was different in a way that made it the same. At the time, I was general counsel to The Human Resources Administration of the City of New York. I was led to believe that the only thing standing in the way of my becoming a partner at Proskauer was the absence of one partner in Europe. As law partnerships are very much private clubs, nothing so radical as the election of a black partner could be consummated without the vote of all the partners. Nevertheless, I felt fairly comfortable. The absent partner had never revealed any animus against me when I was with the firm. Indeed, he had pretty much ignored me. I had had several lunches at the Cornell Club to meet various people then with the firm, and I had had conversations with Walter Mendelsohn, who is the senior senior partner. After the lapse of what seemed a long time, I began to ask how things were going. Silver seemed embarrassed and said little. Finally, Phil Haberman told me that one of his partners, Charles Looker, had said that Negroes were anti-Semitic, that they wanted black power and that then was not the time to take a black partner.

Silver said that, one day, he would try again, but I felt that he did not really mean it and was seeking to offer me a comfort of sorts. It was never to come to pass. However, the time that I had spent at the Proskauer firm was instructive. When, in 1951, I decided to leave that office, I was summoned to the office of Joseph M. Proskauer. I was in awe of him, not only because of his status in the firm, but because he had been a State Supreme Court justice and had served on its Appellate Division.

Proskauer was a remarkably gifted man with a brilliant mind and no tolerance for mediocrity. He demanded to know why I was leaving and asked me if I had any clients. He then said that it was silly to try to start a practice without clients. He then called his secretary and asked her the name of the only client he had when he decided to be independent. He said he had been foolish enough to think he could earn a living with but a single client. At the same time she answered, he said, "Oh, yes, it was that goddamned bank."

He then proceeded to tell me how lucky I was and how things had changed since he was a youth. He began to reminisce about the past, suggesting that just a few years earlier I would never have been fortunate enough to become a lawyer. He told me that his father had been a Confederate colonel and had been wounded by a "Yankee ball" that went through one of his cheeks and out the other. "But my father," he added, "never lost his cigar."

All I could think of was what havoc must have been wrought to his father's teeth and gums. I thought that would be the end of my extraordinary audience, but the judge then recalled his boyhood in Mobile, Alabama. He said that if he was walking along a sidewalk and an approaching Negro did not step deferentially into the roadway or gutter, he had the right to knock him there with impunity. I wondered what would happen if a Negro woman did not defer.

It was an eerie moment, as I thought how strange it felt to be in the presence of a man whose father had fought to preserve black slavery. My own experience with Jews and their involvement in civil rights struggles made it odd for me to remember that there had been Jewish Confederates. In law school, of course, there had been some passing reference to *Benjamin on Sales*, a leading text on the subject. Judah Benjamin had been the Jewish Secretary of State in the Confederacy. There were others, as well, who were ardent Southerners and who identified with the cause of the South during, before and after the Civil War.

History reveals that Morris J. Raphael, a southern rabbi, sought to make certain that American Judaism worked to oppose abolition. He believed that slaveholding was no sin and that the Old Testament could be cited in support of that institution. On the other hand, there were northern Jews who, with equal ardor, supported the Union cause. I had never associated Jews with slaveowning, although there had been some who owned blacks, even as there had been a few Negro slaveowners.

As I sat with the judge, it was a rare and memorable confrontation with history for me. On the one or two other occasions when I had been in the same room with him, he had never spoken directly to me. On one, I was delivering some important papers to him at The Harmony Club where he sat chatting with

47

former Mayor Fiorello LaGuardia. He accepted the papers but never stopped talking with LaGuardia. It was my last sight of LaGuardia. He sat like a round Buddha, smoking, with cigarette ashes strewn down his vest.

Before excusing me and wishing me well, the judge autographed a pen and ink drawing of himself and gave it to me. It was thus that I joined three other young lawyers in a small office on Fifth Avenue at 43rd Street, to begin that adventure known as private practice. The practice itself was uneventful. Because I had been associated with the Proskauer firm, I became known as a "library lawyer," and was subjected to some friendly jeers by various Harlem lawyers. They nevertheless came to me when they wanted a brief written or an appeal argued.

It was a time when most of the black lawyers in Manhattan were clustered in offices at 209 West 125th Street. Several worked full-time for the post office and practiced only at those things that could be done in the office. The practical wisdom was that if a black lawyer had a negligence case that was worth a great deal of money, he would retain a white lawyer of counsel. After all, there were then no more than four black judges in the City at that time and none of them was a Supreme Court justice. My early days at the bar saw my office do the same thing, and Emile Zola Berman was a favorite practitioner to whom our best negligence cases would be referred. The business of my firm took a rather quirky turn in 1952.

One of my clients was Leonard Bates, who had been a great scholar-athlete at New York University during the days when its football team played interstate rivals. Whenever N.Y.U. played a team south of Pennsylvania, however, Bates was left behind, so as not to offend the other team. It was ironic, since offending a football adversary was and is at the heart of the game. It was the kind of racism that famous educational institutions helped perpetuate by accepting it and being willing co-conspirators.

One of the Bates brothers had married a woman from a well-known Boston family. She was one of several beneficiaries of two trust funds and had what is generally described as an independent income. She interested herself in the Bahai faith and the spiritual unity of mankind. She took her four young daughters off to the Caribbean and then to Mexico City. Eventually, she committed suicide and Bates had to go to Mexico City to bring the young children to New York.

In representing Bates, who became the guardian of his brother's daughters, one of my duties had been to go to Mexico to see if I could discover the unmarked grave of the mother of the little girls. The girls themselves had been placed in a private school near Poughkeepsie in upstate New York.

On one weekend, one of the young girls, with other teenagers, came to New York and visited a jazz club where Art Blakey and The Jazz Messengers were performing in Greenwich Village. Blakey and the young girl were soon thereafter married and, as Blakey needed legal advice, I began doing legal work for him. Recognized as one of the two or three great jazz percussionists in the world, he was much in demand in jazz and recording circles, both in the United States and Europe and Japan. After years of classical violin study and being snobbish about Bach, Mozart, Beethoven and others, I began to marvel at the amazements of jazz, and traveled, as Blakey put it, "over three-quarters of the world" with the Jazz Messengers.

Other than my adventures with that group and with other great performers (written about elsewhere), my private practice of law was fairly ordinary. There were members of the Proskauer firm who would refer to me the problems of their maids and other black domestics. It was not a practice calculated to make me a wealthy man, for I had neither negligence nor criminal cases. However, I did enough business to have a great deal of time to myself and to travel with the musicians, as well as to survive the amercements of marriages that did not prosper.

In 1967, members of Mayor John Lindsay's talent scouting

team visited my office to recruit me for public service, something that I had steadfastly rejected during the 1950's. I became general counsel to The Human Resources Administration and started along the road that was to lead, surprisingly, to a career on the bench and exposure to years of controversy and dispute.

While I was not unaware of racism in American society, it was only after I came to the bench that the accumulation of historical data and common experience received a more anxious focus. What follows are some of the details of my thoughts about the judicial system and the racism of America that spills over into that aspect of existence that purports to epitomize impartiality, objectivity and fairness. These, then, are reflections and musings, if you will, on a view of America based upon an entire life spent as a black male in a white world. Nearly one-quarter of that life has been spent as a judge.

***

There are blacks in America who doubtless have some close emotional kinship with successful blacks in South Africa. It is not that American blacks join in violent suppression of other blacks, as do some of the black policemen and soldiers in South Africa. However, there are many so-called successful blacks in America whose notions of conservative existence reflect some of the same values as the most conservative whites. Adam Clayton Powell, Jr., Harlem's first black member of Congress, led demonstrations in the area's main business street, in an effort to compel F. W. Woolworth and other merchants to hire blacks. The people who joined such public and sometimes raucous demonstrations were not those who imagined that they were the cream of black society. They were the urban peasants who heard in Powell's voice a dramatization of their innermost thoughts and fearful longings.

The bane of black progress in America has been the burden of imagined respectability. But it is precisely the respectability of the white majority that has resisted change in racial and racist attitudes. Blacks who claim respectability and allow that mirage to keep them quiet and from being actors in the necessary drama needed to change an oppressive society, are instruments of continued oppression.

And yet, remarkably, there is always some joy to be found in the black American circumstance. It is a perishable joy, to be sure. In its isolation it is given occasional respiration that is as artificial as the dark imitation of American life. Those who bear the scarred beauty of blackness, treasure the surprise of small comforts. We are dreamers who confront visions and nurture illusions and religion. In many ways, blacks are a people without a country and, at the same time, quintessential Americans, second only to the Indians in our miscegenated authenticity. Except for color, the only genetic linkage owned by blacks is with America. And rising from the rich chorus of black music and song, with its joy and its melancholy, is the exquisite sharpness and ironical bite of the black poet, Countee Cullen. In one of his poems, he rebukes God for making a poet black and bidding him to sing.

While many reject the term Negro and prefer black, or Afro-American, few blacks enjoy the luxury of a sturdy bridge to the past. White immigrants celebrate their voluntary exodus from Europe to America. But blacks were never a part of that steerage influx that remembers Ellis Island and the Statue of Liberty with tearful emotion. It is virtually impossible for blacks to look homeward, except with nostalgia for a place they have never been. The critical element of kinship is painfully missing.

While the descendants of white immigrants can return to Europe to visit ancestral villages and relatives, it is difficult to conceive of black Americans dashing off to Africa to visit the old tribe or root families. We have only wonderment for the historical divorce from what we never knew. We cling to America in a

51

pathetic kind of urgency and with the desperation of those without national options.

Black slaves, severed from their tribal sires, became involuntary students of Biblical justification for their American condition. As Anna Arnold Hedgeman reminds us in her book *The Gift of Chaos,* there was a time when Africans were the only immigrants to this country who came without tickets of passage, without visas and without passports and with no sense of direction. Blacks, in their bondage, became an expatriate census, badgered exiles in a world of aliens and citizens without a country. Visionaries and illusionists, their black images of desire fed upon themselves. Public expression of such things invites contempt from both whites and those Afro-Saxons who believe that bitterness is a lack of that gratitude that blacks should feel for America's blessings.

***

The National Lawyers Guild was founded by lawyers who were dissatisfied with the exclusionary establishment. They regarded the American Bar Association as a symbol of toryism. The guild has fought for racial equality throughout the years. Its most successful members, however, have shown little or no interest in having blacks join their firms. At a meeting of the guild to honor one of its founders, Hope Stevens, the black guest speaker publicly mentioned the problem. He reminded the gathering of liberals and left-of-center lawyers and their guests that their proud liberalism and heroic fealty to the civil rights movement had not gone so far as to welcome black lawyers to their law firms. His remarks were received with the stunned silence and embarrassment of a donor of alms who sees the beneficiary of his generosity curse the giver and his gift. It was as though a profane clamor had trespassed in a temple. The brief and hesitant applause that followed was a mere Pavlovian response of an audience programmed to clap at the end of any speech.

No one stood up to challenge Stevens. The membership obviously had no desire for public self-examination or for those dedicatory pledges that spring with guilt. The audience was plainly embarrassed. It was a tribute to the candor of their inbred dedication to the American way of life that none made any false promises to do better. The largely Jewish audience seemed more content to believe that most of them were minorities and that retarding circumstance had not stopped their own progress and that, therefore, blacks should not whine or whimper but do exactly as they had done. Such an angry reaction ignored the fact that Jews, no matter what else Christian America may think of them, have protective coloration, the most blessed of American physical characteristics. It was simply that the audience was humiliated for a moment by the harshness of the truth to which its members had contributed. It was almost as though Stevens had undraped an indecent statute in the presence of prudes who did not realize that they were the sculptors.

Whites, even liberal whites, are weaned on racism. They live and breathe the superiority of options, choices, and opportunities that are available to those who wear the white skin.

When most white students study sociology, it is little more than an academic subject to be passed. The black victims of that social science may be deplored briefly, but they are not to be associated with, understood, or invited to join clubs and fraternities. When they graduate into professional schools and careers, whites carry these exclusions into their professions.

Law schools of today appear to believe in more and more practical clinical programs. Their students are now placed with judges and administrators of private and government affairs. Few schools, however, place their students in black slum areas, where they can touch, taste and experience life in living color, or at least try to do so.

I say "try," because I believe, with James Baldwin, that perhaps no white will ever be able to feel the debasement reserved for dark skin in America until some white is compelled by general circumstance to write a song such as the Negro spiritual, "Sometimes I Feel Like a Motherless Child."

White liberals are, naturally, a failure if their liberalism is supposed to stand for anything meaningful to blacks. It is as though they have a special definition for blacks, which has built-in limitations. It reaches a point at which it satisfies its own restricted meaning and, after that, the metamorphosis allows each liberal to deteriorate into a white John Average. Along with blacks, then, they recognize that majority rule must carry the day and that blacks in a white society are at the mercy of those who outnumber them. As with the Jews, who should be their natural allies in a Christian country of potential jeopardy, the blacks are the most endangered of all endangered species.

It is clear that many blacks believe that Jews should be their allies. Those who cherish such a fugitive concept are mistaken. In America, Jews have found the flawed but almost perfect sociopolitical ecology for their development and prosperity. They are accepted as white, the historical precondition for American success. In New York, at least, since the 1930s, Jews have dominated the legal profession by numbers alone. Accepted by both the American Bar Association and the Association of the Bar of the City of New York long before blacks, many have risen to positions of preeminence in the profession.

One of my Jewish friends, now a senior managing partner in a prestigious and wealthy law firm, once said to me with a pleased smile, "Well, Bruce, the Jews are now deans of the four most important law schools in the country." He was speaking proudly of Harvard, Yale, Cornell, and Columbia. He could see no danger in that success and ridiculed my expressed fear that society could turn against the Jews. He refused to believe that in America the Jews could ever join the blacks as an endangered species. It made no difference to him that the Nazis were Christians, both Protestants and Catholics, as were the overwhelming numbers of slaveowners in America.

With so numerous a census of Jewish lawyers, from among whom so many judges are selected, one might expect that the New York bench would be one of the most liberal in the world. It might be expected that Jewish judges and lawyers—aware of who had been the chief victims of Nazi judges, lawyers, and law—would be avid guardians of the law to make certain that it never faltered in its high purpose of evenhanded libertarianism. There would be a certain degree of self-interested morality in assuring equality to the blacks so that nothing sinister could befall the Jews.

I cherished this hapless vision for many years. When I was practicing law, I assumed that the only way to win a fair hearing for my black clients was to appear before a Jewish judge. I ridiculed those who changed their religion from Christian to Moslem, suggesting that it made more sense to become a Jew. Whenever any case of mine came before an Irish Catholic judge or the one or two Protestant judges then sitting, I would not hesitate to adjourn it, in the hope of coming before two of the Jewish judges my preference it was to argue before, either Henry Clay Greenberg or Samuel Hofstadter. Their reputations were a guarantee that close attention would be paid to the merits without regard to the race of the lawyer of the client. In my view, however, both made typical white American mistakes in cases that were disputes involving acute issues of pure racism.

In a suit against the Hotel Pierre for the Urban League Guild, there had been victory at the trial level. On appeal before the Appellate Term of the Supreme Court, Hofstadter posed questions that revealed how distant was his understanding of discrimination resting solely upon race. Mrs. Molly Moon was the tireless head of the guild, a fund-raising arm of the league. She had arranged by telephone for the guild's annual summer fund-raising party to be held on the Hotel Pierre's roof garden, and she appeared in person to sign the contract. The banquet manager, obviously taken aback when he saw that she was a black woman, refused to deal with her. He denied that he had spoken to her by telephone or that the date and alternative date discussed had ever been available. Because the guild is composed of blacks and whites, Hofstadter said that the civil rights law was not meant to cover such situations. He said that Mrs. Moon was the agent of an interracial principal and could have no relief.

I said to him, "Your Honor, assume that you, a white person, asked me, a Negro, to get a container of coffee for you. I go to the restaurant and ask for the coffee. The counterman says to me, 'Bruce, you know we don't serve colored people here.' I reply, 'But this is for Judge Hofstadter, not me.' Under those circumstances, do you mean to suggest that there is no discrimination against me because of my color?" Judge Hofstadter was so discomfited that he spun around in his swivel chair and said, "Come, now, Mr. Wright. When one Negro is discriminated against, you want to give every Negro in the country a cause of action."

I replied, somewhat testily, that that might not be a bad idea. In an unprecedented reaction by the Appellate Term audience, there was brief and surprising applause.

Later in my career, one of the respected judges of the Civil Court requested that I write an opinion for him in another hotel discrimination case. I did so, taking the opportunity to attack the reasoning in the Molly Moon case and making it clear that the civil rights law should also cover whites who were discriminated against because of color. In the latter case, a white wife and a black husband had been refused accommodations because, as the hotel manager said, "Mixed couples always fight."

In the area of criminal law, it is difficult to imagine more than a few Jewish judges before whom a black defendant might appear in the hope, not of favoritism, but simply of a fair and unbiased hearing into which innate racism would not intrude. One of the problems is that white judges fail to perceive a color problem that lies deep within themselves and is the grotesque product of their daily lives from the time they are born.

Americans are victims of a problem that has mistakenly been characterized as "the Negro Problem" but is really a white one, deeply rooted in traditional racism. One of the oddities in American life, both ironic and paradoxical, is that blacks, who were once deprived of education deliberately and then given inferior instruction, understand perfectly the folly and senselessness of color discrimination, yet whites seem to be increasingly dense on the subject.

My Jewish friends, for example, utterly fail to understand the fallacious opposition to what they call racial quotas. They prefer to recall that Jews themselves were victims of quotas, especially at the so-called Ivy League universities and at U.S. medical schools. But they forget that they made up those quotas at prestigious schools to which blacks had no entree at all. They also neglect to comprehend a striking distinction between the restrictive quotas imposed on them in the past (and probably in the present in some cases) and those devised by some courts to open and expand opportunities for blacks.

There is a vast difference between quotas that limit and those that expand, in order, as the argument goes, to redress past discriminations, which are not really past at all. The plight of Jews and blacks should be seen as more similar than different. Although the Jews fought against discriminatory quotas, they accepted them by enrolling whenever they could. The blacks accepting quotas of expansion also are struggling to come from behind and in greater numbers. They also want a system of merit, but they want it to start in the earliest grade school years of instruction, so that all black neighborhood schools do not become the neglected academic orphans of the system.

The Christian society's imposition of Jewish quotas should

have long ago conveyed the ominous message of America's blood-based caste system. Despite what happened in Nazi Germany, even in the postwar period in America, many universities in this country still had Jewish quotas. When John Sloan Dickey was the president of Dartmouth College, he felt so secure in the tradition of Christian hegemony that he could candidly announce that, yes, Dartmouth did have quotas for Jewish students and that these quotas were for the benefit of the Jews; there would be less discrimination if there were smaller numbers of such students on campus. For an educator to have such a view smacks of a grave gap in his education.

Christian racists must be amused to see the blacks and Jews pitted against each other. Nearly all of the most powerful Jewish organizations brought their considerable resources together to oppose black aspirations for entry into professional and graduate schools, as well as for new opportunities in industry. The industrial disputes found the Jewish ideologues in a particularly offensive posture because they well knew of the oppressive cooperation between unions and management through the years to deprive blacks of chances for advancement. They should have known how demeaning it is to blacks to be compelled to fight for quotas. The sociological warfare had sometimes escalated into street riots for the sparse improvements in life that eventually were won. That dark struggle is not aided by those who scream about quotas, preferential treatment, and reverse discrimination.

No one seems to understand that inherent in the term "reverse discrimination" is the discrimination that blacks have sought to reverse since the bias imposed by the Constitution. Jews should remember that the Constitution never referred to them as "three-fifths of a person," nor did it speak of their "importation." Blacks may be able to hate, to detest, to dislike, and to express bitter opinions, but seldom are they in positions to discriminate, that is, to deprive some other person of a merited advantage because of race, color, national origin, or religion.

A recent letter to *The New York Times*, signed by one Miro M. Todorovich, illustrates how white immigrants often seek to outdo native Americans in committing fouls in the skin game. With an apparently straight face, Todorovich seeks to defend Mayor Edward Koch's opposition to the 10 percent set aside for minority contracts as upheld by the United States Supreme Court. The letter-writer concludes his paean of praise for Koch by admonishing the congressional Black Caucus to "ponder the wisdom of seeking reparations at the expense of enterprises that built this nation with hard work and the spirit of competition."

Such crass and racist ignorance of history is unforgivable in one who describes himself as a professor at a community college. He ignores the disgraceful panorama of black slavery and the fact that those slaves also "built this nation with hard work." Theories of competition were ruled out because they could only have advanced the slaves and would have involved no reparations such as were paid to the Jewish survivors of the Nazi Holocaust and are being sought by the Japanese survivors of America's World War II concentration camps and by dispossessed Indians, victims of patriotic grand larceny of their geography by pious white settlers. I daresay Todorovich might oppose reparations payable to those blacks who were able to prove their genetic kinship with unpaid slaves.

3

Judging the Judges

The battles of blacks have always been waged under adverse circumstances. Even their purported allies and friends have difficulty understanding the ambition of blacks to be ordinary Americans. Black hope is opposed with such fierce energy and massed resources that new terms have had to be invented, so that black zeal is now said to be synonymous with reverse discrimination.

Yet there is little reason for such a lack of understanding. Through their lawsuits for citizen rights, blacks have made U.S. Supreme Court rulings the common knowledge of even the most benighted whites, including white criminal court judges. The black struggle has been obscure, despite its well-dressed politesse and its syllables of reason. In effect, blacks have by their lawsuits run a coast-to-coast classroom in which they have sought to teach whites the true and humanitarian meaning of their own invention of democracy.

White America, however, seems to have been a reluctant student. The numerous and famous victories of Thurgood Marshall in the Supreme Court, before he became a member of that court, should have shown the country the great distance between blacks and equality. Instead, many whites began to believe that blacks were far ahead. The only reason for such a belief had be that whites have a restricted "place" for blacks, a point beyond which dark citizenship should not be permitted to go.

At the height of Thurgood Marshall's triumphs as an NAACP lawyer, a joke among the black literati said that the amended Constitution was God, Thurgood was its prophet, and the justices of the Supreme Court were the Nine Old Disciples. But all of that changed, and the change took place just before the turbulent demonstrations of the 1960s, which revealed American apartheid as a latter-day emperor and his new clothing.

The charismatic mythology that surrounded John F. Kennedy led to the belief that he was an ally of black advancement. Timid civil rights legislation had been proposed as though a generous gift of national resources was being handed over to blacks. The cry was heard throughout the land that "the niggers have too much," thus emphasizing how little they had and how little society wished them to have. After he telephoned the prison where Dr. Martin Luther King, Jr., was being held, President Kennedy achieved a reputation as a civil libertarian and as a kind of adoptive father of civil rights. But even he felt it necessary to say at one point that there were enough civil rights laws on the books. Perhaps he was correct, or would have been, had the Fourteenth Amendment been honored by the Congress of the United States as an example for the rest of white America. Laws have all too often been construed away from forceful meaning and been no more than decorative icing on a befouled national cake.

Despite endowing the Constitution's emancipatory amendments, black life is a constant ordeal, and the country is akin to a private club with glorious opportunities, options, and choices for white and, more recently, Oriental immigrants. Because Fidel Castro's Caribbean communism was regarded as subversive, all that the mostly white Cubans had to do to be welcomed with open arms was to flee a government that was automatically regarded as red and oppressive.

Black Haitian refugees, however, were tossed back into the sea, and those who remained were introduced to the ghost of the Dred Scott syndrome by having to sue for human rights in a country that invented them. Black immigrants continue to have their American problems, including limited quotas. Still, they may be better off than those blacks who came here for sale.

People who remain insensitive to the constitutional aspirations of black citizens have nevertheless found enough humanitarian enthusiasm to welcome foreign refugees, without remembering that black Americans are themselves refugees in their own land.

A. Leon Higginbotham, Jr., has issued the first of several projected volumes dealing with the historical roots of racism in the American legal process. It is a thoroughly researched and incisive scholarship, illuminating Americana that has long been buried in obscure archives. America prefers to remember the cherry tree mythology and the I-Cannot-Tell-a-Lie apocrypha of George Washington rather than his Christian devotion to slaveowning.

Children are taught in school that John Marshall was the greatest chief justice the land has ever had, but not that on his tenth birthday he received a black slave as a gift and that upon his marriage he received another. The country thinks loving and compassionate thoughts of Robert E. Lee and even of his beloved horse, Traveler, but not that he was a traitor to the Union, who led the bloodiest rebellion ever known to America. Both a nuclear submarine and a university are named in Lee's dubious honor.

In these pages, I have no intention of reviewing the history that is detailed in the Higginbotham work. Neither will I rewrite the work of Derrick A. Bell, Jr., formerly a black professor at the Harvard Law School. He has written a praiseworthy book, *Race, Racism and American Law*. It is much easier to read than the Higginbotham book and perhaps more effective in its impact. My purpose here is to concentrate on racism in New York, which, for the most part, as I read national press stories, does not seem to be vastly different from that in any other part of the country.

Discrimination today is more urbane than the raw racism of the pre-1960s; that is, Americans often camouflage their racism. With the coming of the civil rights legislation of the 1960s, the country entered upon a more subtle discover-the-loophole era. It is no longer fashionable for otherwise sane whites to call blacks niggers. The game has now become discovering ways to treat them that way with impunity.

Berlioz's opera *The Judges of the Secret Court* is more than merely the title of a musical work. It depicts daily reality in many ways. The Criminal Courts Building at 100 Centre Street in Manhattan is an exemplar of the incompatibility of architecture and acoustics.

Mr. Justice Owen McGivern, a former presiding justice of the Appellate Division of the New York State Supreme Court, is a man of keen wit. In voicing an opinion about the design and structure of 100 Centre Street, he once remarked that, when Harry K. Thaw shot Stanford White, the wrong architect was killed. The courtrooms there are secret because what goes on at the bench is seldom heard beyond that immediate area unless a judge elects to exercise his royal prerogative to scream. And yet, what goes on at the bench constitutes the vitals of the entire system. There, the prosecutor, defense counsel, and judge have quiet and earnest discussions. There, plea bargains are struck; the question of what sentence is to be imposed is decided or agreed upon; the amount of a fine is determined; and the urgings of judicial mercy are made.

More often than not, the name of the judge is not posted on the bench or elsewhere. Practically anonymous prisoners or defendants come before an unknown judge. It is amazing how many defendants never know the name of the person who can, and often does, drastically affect their lives, their freedom, and their fortune. Many never know the name of the prosecutor who zealously seeks to abort such freedom as they have. And even more sadly, the poor defendants who rely upon appointed counsel often never know the names of the lawyers who are the trustees of their destiny or doom. They have come to believe that everything is predetermined and that nothing a defendant can do will make any difference.

It is a mock pageant, they believe and, without knowing Dante Alighieri's *Divine Comedy*, they have nevertheless instinctively adopted the motto "Abandon all hope, ye who enter here." The gossip of the cell is that the more one resembles the judge, the more likely is the chance for justice or a break. Since upward of 90 percent of the judges are white and 85 to 90 percent of the criminal court defendants are black or dark Hispanics, the chance of such a break is immediately defined.

There are black judges who are so godly in their dark ascendance, so remote in the social distance they imagine separates them from their kith and kin of melanin, that they joyously believe themselves to be charter members of the black bourgeoisie. Status-conscious impostors by self-anointment, they are so white in their imitation of life and in their reactions to black defendants that they are known as "Afro-Saxons."

They are black judges in skin color only. They fail to understand that if there is no difference between white and black judges, there is no need to emphasize the paucity of black judges or the deliberate exclusion of black lawyers from the bench through the use of limiting quotas. Although the labor force and even police departments can have court-ordered racial proportions so that black membership in public or private employment can reflect racial population percentages, no such attention has ever been focused on judges. Thus, appointing officials are always able to hide behind their "discretion," their emphasis on "merit" and those who are "qualified."

This discretion serves the purpose of severely restricting the number of blacks on the bench, while at the same time perpetuating the myth that black lawyers are not qualified for judging. Among the few black judges who do sit, there are those who have come, in many cases, to feel that they belong to an exclusive club of special adjuncts of the system, selected because of their natural superiority. Such loftiness and imagined standing are intensified when these judges fail to regard with concern the absence of Hispanic judges, whose numbers are even fewer than those of blacks.

Black judges seldom if ever speak out on controversial subjects. They maintain a low profile, wearing at all times the mask of mute and well-behaved dignity. They are as well dressed as funeral directors. They know their obscure place, which is special only in the black society in which they circulate. Criminal Court judges in New York City know and fully appreciate that they are at the mercy of the mayor who appoints them or whoever is in office at the time of possible reappointment. A low, cautious, and obedient profile will ensure their survival. To the extent that they do the mayor's bidding, or at least do not offend his standards for judging, they remain "qualified," both to sit and to be reappointed.

Mayor Edward Koch is fairly typical of those whites who are fond of having orchestrated what they refer to as a "liberal" past. Having been elected with the help of the city's large black population, he has had many opportunities to show his true colors. None has been overlooked.

Judging the Judges

Mayor Koch's appointment of blacks to the Criminal Court has been almost wholly limited to the reappointment of those whose terms began under earlier mayors. He has reserved the right to criticize publicly any judge whose rulings offend his personal sense of the law he has not practiced or the judging he has never done. In addition to revealing himself as a doctrinaire ideologue, his claimed liberal spirit has been confined to his scathing statements that have been directed at both black and white, male and female judges.

Such pandering to public fear ensures his popularity among those who have only minimal regard for the Constitution, but such inflammatory arrogance undermines confidence in the administration of justice generally. This is strange and hostile conduct for one who, as Koch does, holds a law degree, and who is the city's chief magistrate.

Koch has exhibited a waspish allegiance to cruel adjectives. He speaks of his own pride in being a Jew but can discover no reason for black pride. I neither obeyed nor sought to discover his uncodified standards of judging. To do so would be to abdicate the office of judging and be little more than an obeisant puppet.

After my ten stormy years on the Criminal Court, the mayor allowed rumor to leak the message that I would not be reappointed. His Committee on the Judiciary did not respond to the voluminous forms I had filled and delivered to it as proof of my interest in reappointment. Despite my approval by watchdog bar association committees and civil libertarians, no official word ever emanated from the office of the mayor.

When he was still a congressman, Koch had written a harshly critical article condemning me as a judge. Because of my part in a bail controversy involving Joseph Grutolla, a white man who had been accused of shooting a police officer and a patron of a bar (also white), he urged my dismissal from the bench. He was aided in his bitter attack by a lack of knowledge of the facts.

Although he was perhaps launching his ambitions to be mayor of New York, those who had believed him to be the liberal he claimed to be were shocked by his intemperate outburst. By the strangeness of coincidence that defies fictitious invention, both Koch and I were hosts at that time for the Fortune Society at a fund-raising affair at the Harvard Club. The executive director of Offender Aid Restoration, of which I was then a vice-president, sought to speak to Koch. She asked him how he could write such a harshly critical article without knowing the facts. With an impetuous toss of his head and with his nose in the air, Koch gave her a withering look and walked away without a word.

His article, written in February 1973, covered three columns in the *Westsider*, a Manhattan newspaper. It appeared to urge that the state legislature adopt preventive detention, so that anyone accused of shooting a police officer be held in minimum bail of $25,000 (inflation since that time has doubtless increased that sum ten-fold). The good congressman, of that time fell into the same error that is common among those whose blood lust persuades them that there must be a death penalty for the murder of a police officer.

It is precisely that arbitrary determination that a police officer's life has greater value than that of anyone else which has been cited as a flaw in the constitutionality of death penalty statutes. Koch had written his angry little essay in response to a letter to the *Westsider* accusing him of "appealing to right-wing bigotry based on fear and ignorance." The letter was from Elizabeth Most, who is white.

The New York Civil Liberties Union, in which Koch claimed membership, had criticized the then congressman for urging my removal from the bench. It had lumped him with Mayor Lindsay, who had expressed "dismay" over my bail decisions and described the defendant as a "cold-blooded gunman if there ever was one."

The defendant, a family man who owned two business ventures in Queens, had himself been terribly wounded and was in need of hospital care. The district attorney presented no evidence that the defendant would fail to appear on any adjourned date of the case. I asked him what bail he could afford and that was the bail I set, $500. It was the respect I paid to the prepresumption of innocence that so excited Congressman Koch, Mayor Lindsay, and the then police commissioner, who said that my action was a "disgrace."

The case finally reached the Court of Appeals, after findings of guilt in the lower courts by a jury at trial and by the Appellate Division of the New York State Supreme Court. The seven judges of the Court of Appeals divided four to three on the question of the defendant's guilt. The dissenters called the case one of "horrendous misidentification."

The symmetry of the proof of guilt was never as clear-cut as Congressman Koch had prejudged it to be. In light of political considerations, of course, that circumstance was of no moment. It is assumed that that case and others were very much in his mind when he refused to consider my reappointment to the Criminal Court. He has since made it abundantly clear that he never intended to reappoint me.

Mayor Abraham Beame, who preceded Koch as the city's chief magistrate, had as his closest adviser on the judiciary and appointments to the bench one Milton Gould. Gould firmly believed, and expressed the view publicly, that it was extremely difficult or impossible to find what he referred to as "qualified" blacks for the bench. He was careful never to spell out what constituted a "qualified" black, or whether such qualifications were different from those needed by a white candidate for judicial appointment. One was left to suspect that he meant that blacks should be white.

On paper, the qualifications for being a judge are that one should be a lawyer who has practiced for at least ten years after admission to the Bar. It helps if no atrocious and scandalous complaints have been lodged against one during his or her career. It also helps to be white.

Nelson Rockefeller, through his manipulation of public information experts and a famous smile, managed to persuade citizen opinion that he was a benevolent liberal. It does not speak well for the democracy of so many Republicans that they regarded him as being dangerously left of center. During his sixteen years as governor of New York, he appointed only one black to the bench, Samuel R. Pierce, Jr. It was only after he had passed his notorious and draconian narcotics law that he made several Court of Claims appointments of black judges to sit as acting Supreme Court justices in the special narcotics courts.

There is constant agitation by elitists in government to abandon the elective system in favor of appointing all judges. I suspect that if such a plan is ever adopted there will be even fewer black judges than there are now, for most of them have come to the bench by way of election.

Compelled for the most part to live in their allotted ghettos, blacks have been permitted only the most mendacious and shifting quota of judges, even through the process of elections. This strict limitation works against the possibility of those regarded as activists coming to the bench. The conservatism of governors and mayors having the exclusive right of appointment would serve only to reduce numbers already minuscule. The only way the first black judge in New York was elected was through the creation of a Jim Crow judicial district in Harlem. Under the appointive process those who have the governor's ear are fellow elitists in charge of political power, not blacks. Blacks are seldom close to the hubs of power with whatever persuasiveness they have. As with the liberal white Protestant law firms and the Jewish partner, blacks in government are proud tokens, symbols in their lone presence of the absence of so many others. The only advantage of a politically gerrymandered black residential enclave is the power of its voters to assert their numbers at the polls. Of course, that black power has never been used to its potential.

So cynical have some blacks become over the failures and betrayals of both major parties that they believe they can write off the society that has written them off, by not voting. P. J. Sidney, the black activist and actor, was engaged in civil rights struggles long before it became either relatively safe or fashionable. He has said that the only way blacks will achieve power is if all whites drop dead immediately. He then adds, somewhat wistfully, that that is not likely, given the disparity between white and black death rates.

One day, perhaps, black voters will wake up and insist that their black judges be more responsive to black concerns in a white world and more aware of their obligation to try to teach their white colleagues. A role model of black judges is easily found in Thurgood Marshall, who has never hesitated to speak out, whether by majority opinion or in dissent, on matters of American democracy that need black therapy and the reasoning that supports the best concepts of the Constitution's idealistic amendments.

One thing is certain, and that is that blacks can take no patriotic vengeance against an oppressive system unless they vote. Non-voting is a fruitless temper tantrum. To the extent that blacks refuse to vote they reflect the philosophy of some men's room graffiti, which weep, "If voting would change anything, it would be illegal."

In a conspiracy of defective acoustics and public servants who shrink from all scrutiny, most of the daily decisions of the Criminal Court are made in the privacy of chambers, or at quiet bench conferences. One lawyer or another may ask that certain discussions take place in chambers, in the robing room, or simply off the record. In such totally private sessions, the lawyers and the judge determine a defendant's fate. The defendant is not present until the judge and lawyers return from making their quiet arrangements. Before either the judge or the district attorney says, "On the record," the defendant is consulted briefly and told the consequences of his attorney's negotiations. That is generally the sum of the consultation. As in life outside the courtroom or prison walls, the accused has severely limited options and choices. It helps to be a stoic.

What kind of (mostly) white men and women are these people who preside over such goings-on and, for the most part, believe that they are acting honorably and in the best traditions of their ancient calling? They are middle class, generally either by the material substance they have accumulated through the years or by their affection for genealogy. They are ambitious, yearning for positions of power, advertised respectability, and that prestige they believe themselves entitled to by reason of their self-appraised worth.

No known scandals stain their reputations, although there may be certain domestic suppressions, known to spouses and children, lovers and mistresses. They are moderate citizens who have been politically circumspect and loyal to one or the other of the two main political parties. They probably belong to clubs that would, under no circumstances, admit blacks; some admit no women. If male and hardworking at their practice, they may be a bit disappointed in life and its sometimes small rewards.

They are not Wall Street types, for these generally cover the federal bench or something more worthy of American Bar Association approval. They are seldom, if ever, partners in the large, business-oriented firms, earning $300,000 or $400,000 a year while surrounded by brilliant young associates fawning and competing for attention and most-favored roles as successors apparent in the partnership hierarchy. To justify the ego fed by the average lawyer's eclectic knowledge of small details, the bench often seems a suitable place on which to wind down one's legal career.

Lawyers are a breed apart. They belong to the second oldest profession. If college is the academic cradle of what they know, law school becomes the hammock, strung between theories of human conduct and the reality of what is. Once graduated from law school, they go through the cramming period, during which they condense three years of law school subject matter into a few weeks of preparation for the bar examination.

Former students of professorial arrogance are handed over to down-to-earth moonlighting lawyers who advertise their infallible ability to guess what focal and pivotal questions will be on the examination. They also inoculate their graduates with the belief that they are about to learn how to win a license to practice their durable profession.

This is a period of acute tension and crisis. It becomes harshly intensified after the examination has been taken and one works, while waiting for the results to be published. Whether one's answers are correct within boundaries of established legal precedents is hardly the point. Those who succeed are, more often than not, those who know best how to express the written word. "Who pays any attention/to the syntax of things/will never wholly kiss you," according to e. e. cummings, but in the law, those who do often carry the day. To conquer the treason of words with grace and style of expression gives one's writing that veneer of professionalism which wins the precious license.

Naturally, the bar examination is irrelevant to the crude facts of existence and the causes of those raw controversies that fill up the law court calendars. If the questions were relevant to the reality of daily law practice naggings, such as the afflictions of the black ghetto, then most of those blessed with a Harvard or Yale Law School degree would, like Theseus, be lost in the labyrinth, but without an Ariadne. The theoretical philosophy of law and morals that one gets from brooding professors seldom matches the rough symmetry of life as it is.

Few law schools teach the substance of law for the poor. Those that decided that such innovation is proper find themselves unaccredited and intellectually scorned by organizations that grade by academic standing.

The Antioch Law School in Washington touches this brave new world of legal instruction and is among the first of the few to take a realistic approach to that endurance of hostility known as poverty. Law schools, like law courts, are concerned chiefly with the protection and proprieties of the haves. Both schools and teachers are protectionist. No law school, for example, teaches the rudiments of survival techniques and beating the law, as opposed to discovering loopholes in tax statutes, which benefit the rich.

John DeWitt Gregory, a black professor at Hofstra Law School, is one of the first teachers to revise the order and materials of a subject traditionally known as Creditors' Rights and Remedies. He now conducts a course entitled Debtors' Rights and Remedies. Gregory, a product of Harvard Law School and thus a survivor himself, has been aided by the humanitarian quondam dean of Hofstra Law School, Monroe Friedman.

Most of us who come to the bar are deeply concerned about our standing as professionals. We treasure our imagined status in society. Pretensions seem to be a necessary substitute for the abolition of titles of nobility in our democratic society. So ritualized has our public conduct become that the people of the commonwealth are persuaded to believe that some persons actually "look like lawyers." The pomp and *trompe l'oeil* of appearances are often symbolized by a three-piece suit, a certain arrogance of posture and stride, and the obligatory briefcase, preferably of genuine leather, or, if not, of a product as deceptive as one's manner.

The pinstripe, asserted but not forced against a dark fabric, suggests taste. Artificial buttonholes at the jacket cuffs and at least three useless buttons endow the suit with an equally artificial class and tone. Designer glasses heighten the overall impression.

One must have an aura of superiority to justify the high fees charged to those who consult such an elegant guru of legal secrets. If one is fortunate, such pomp may induce sufficient awe to assure prompt payment. The latter is a vital part of upward mobility in the law business and of ultimately removing one's office from a humble origin to a prestigious address. Many of the white judges who early assert a right to be regarded as experts on blacks, because so many of their clients are black, have relied on fees paid by their socially scorned clientele as a means of abandoning the city and moving to some racially pure haven in the suburbs.

Lawyers who live in Brooklyn (mostly Brooklyn Heights), and who claim to be practitioners of elegance and substance, seldom have office addresses in that borough and especially not on Court Street, where many undistinguished attorneys are thought to be.

In Manhattan, 305 Broadway used to be known as "the Den of Forty Thieves," reflecting the appearance of the building and the snobbish opinion of lawyers located elsewhere on lower Broadway. This was not because the doctors *juris* there were any worse than any other lawyers, but because the structure was regarded as a law office slum.

A mystical quality surrounds the term "Wall Street lawyer," even though many of the most prestigious firms long ago moved to Park Avenue and even Third Avenue. When such lawyers win cases, the reason invariably given is their thorough and expert preparation. When others win, they are cursed by the adjective "clever." Black lawyers, when triumphant, are all too often described as "lucky."

The excellence of preparation and the high quality of the work

75

product attributed to prestigious firms become a problem when lawyers from two such firms oppose each other. Only one can win; there are few draws in legal competition. In such cases, the firm that takes the prize is generally said to have been "better connected" than the other, either politically or in ways that are never revealed. Paul, Weiss, Rifkind, Wharton & Garrison is often described as one of the most powerful and influential firms in the country. The firm of Shea, Gould, Climenko & Casey (now simply Shea Gould) enjoys a similar reputation.

Descriptions of law firms tend to neglect the question of merit. It is grossly unfair to judges to suggest that one party wins because his counsel is "well connected," for the implication is that "connections," not a fair trial, carried the day.

Aspersions are also cast on both counsel and the bench, suggesting less than a proper trial.

There is little doubt, however, that many judges are overawed by the large, wealthy firms, especially when these are opposed by a single practitioner. Seldom if ever do wealthy Wall Street lawyers forego their rich practices to accept appointment to the bench of the Criminal Court. Rather the bench of the lower courts is usually representative of the less prosperous members of the bar.

How are judges selected for appointment or nominated for election? I have been both appointed and elected. In many ways, I am an accidental judge. At the time I came to the bench, I had absolutely no experience in criminal law, except that I had argued appeals of cases that had already been tried. Mayor Lindsay said he wanted a fresh approach, which could be best achieved by someone who was unknown at the trial level.

I had never been a member of a political club and, indeed, at the time of my appointment, was not registered in a party. I was clearly not selected for appointment for any of the reasons I suggest for determining judicial merit. Such a determination is difficult at best because no institution exists to train lawyers to be judges.

The career is one of on-the-job training and experience. Such experience can be educational in ways never taught or dreamed of in the world of academia. A judge, never before exposed to the shocking underside of life, becomes educated when he learns of the separate world in which people exist by theft, burglary, rape, mugging and, sometimes, murder.

Some judges become hardened to the daily pageant paraded before them by the police and devote themselves to the political goals of seeking promotion and advancement within the system. From them no outcry of criticism is ever heard. They become assembly-line workers to whom the defendants cease to be individuals, either worthy or unworthy of an attempt at understanding or rehabilitation. People become things to be arranged in categories dictated by the charges.

As in chess, a flawed move earns an inescapable consequence. When the legal system separates people from the shape and essence of humanity, it deprives itself of the right to use the term "justice." As dust is swept beneath a carpet by a careless housecleaner, so too are some defendants swept into prison.

The longer I remained on the Criminal Court bench, the more I wondered why lawyers would forego the freedom of practice and the unfettered right of free speech to accept employment in a system that monitors conduct so closely. On those occasions when I have been before disciplinary committees, it has always been for speaking my mind, instead of minding my speech.

It is almost as though judges are to be no more than well-behaved automatons, enjoined from engaging in controversial comments in public. And yet they are called upon every day to sit in judgment of the most contentious disputes and to favor one side or another as a matter of public record. Controversy, indeed, defines the necessity for judicial arbitration and peaceful judgments.

It must be difficult for a lawyer-become-judge to pacify his or her normal instincts to identify with controversy. This is especially true of judges who have come to judging by way of long membership in a political club. There are always internal disputes in such clubs, and district leaders are always vulnerable to insurgent dissidents lining up their forces for a coup.

In such cases, a lawyer must take sides and become an advocate of his selected leader. One's own private ambition to become a judicial officer can depend on the success of that leader. Leaders of political clubs take great pleasure in wielding their power to recommend the election or appointment of judges or municipal government commissioners.

Being a judge alters one's visible personality. For some time, the administrative judge for the Brooklyn branch of the state supreme court was a black man, William Thompson, known as Willie to his intimates. Colloquial and tough in expression and politically well connected, he once relished his role as a kingmaker. He does not pretend to possess any of the intellectual graces. His totem is raw political power. Once he said that he was content to remain a kingmaker, a behind-the-scenes activist.

Thompson professed to dislike the tame, restricted, and unexciting life of a judge. Judges are barred by judicial canons from any partisan political activity. When the opportunity arose, however, the magic power of judging was too powerful for him to resist. He decided that he no longer wished to be responsible for the judicial elevation of others when he could promote himself. He seems now to prefer the magisterial life of a judge, regardless of its sedentary duties. In 1980, he was promoted to the appellate division of the state supreme court.

So powerful is this black politician-become-judge that his administrative position was not heady enough. He is said to have

dared the ultimate taboo of those whites who permitted his elevation to the bench: he has allied himself in marriage to one of
the few women in the courts, a white judge. Such a brazen capit-
ulation to passion and human emotions may present a stern challenge to his friends, who believe that they are liberals.

For the moment, Thompson is one of the preferred token
blacks in Brooklyn. So Afro-Saxon is he that he has not hesitated
publicly to accuse me of being a racist. In 1978, I was the
speaker at a dinner of the Kings County Criminal Bar Association. My subject was the vexatious matter of racism. I spoke of
the sorry disparity in sentencing, noting that black defendants
often received much harsher sentences than whites convicted of
identical crimes. I also mentioned that women of all colors were
treated little better than blacks and that the small number of
blacks on the bench proved that racial limitations plagued our
learned profession.

When I concluded, a white law secretary to a supreme court
justice leaped to his feet and practically screamed, "That's racist
crap; that's all that is: that's garbage!"

During my speech, Thompson had chatted incessantly and
audibly with his female companion. He had obviously heard
very little I had said. Nevertheless, he too, leaped to his feet
and, with one arm raised in a gesture of angry defiance, he
looked at me and yelled, "That's right; that's nothing but racist
garbage."

Clearly, some blacks do not believe there is any taint of racism
in our system. Such blacks, naturally, become the beneficiaries
of liberal whites. The deceitful ploy of making noncontroversial
and "acceptable" blacks deputized administrators in the judicial
system is one way of camouflaging the disgraceful near-absence
of black and Puerto Rican judges. Many blacks, who notice the
system, have long realized that black tokens appointed by the
whites in power must be carefully watched, for they all too often
seem to forget that they are black. Not so is Milton Williams,

who has defied several stereotypes. Now administrative judge for the New York City courts, both criminal and civil, he was formerly a police officer. He brings to his position an uncommon understanding of both judges and judging.

The political poverty of blacks is not always symbolized by the system's adoption of the Willie Thompsons. But if blacks are ever to have more than symbolic recognition, black voters must express the power of their numbers. Persuading black voters to exercise the ballot has thus far been a lost cause in New York, as elsewhere other than the South since the 1960s.

When asked why he is reluctant to vote, the black man in the street will generally say that it only helps the so-called middle-class blacks to get token positions after which they move out of the ghetto and forget who helped them realize their ambitions. Consequently, tokenism will continue to be the rule.

Now and then, somehow, blacks of exceptional merit manage to retain the respect and affection of the ghetto community. One of those was James S. Watson, the first black judge in the history of New York. An immigrant from Spanish Town, Jamaica, he was a man of remarkable gifts as both lawyer and judge. Until his death he remained a resident of Harlem. If pure merit had received its just reward, he would have sat as a member of this country's highest court. He was a model of the idealist's vision of what a judge should be in both humanitarian and intellectual concepts.

When I was still a law student, he often allowed me to discuss with him some of the more interesting and intellectually demanding conflicts that came before the court over which he presided.

I saw an example of how racial politics can affect a man's career one night in 1948, when I was visiting Judge Watson in his study. A group of white men was ushered in. They looked at me suspiciously through their cigar smoke, made a few quiet remarks to Judge Watson, and retreated to another room of the handsome brownstone house. About fifteen minutes later, the judge returned. There were tears in his eyes. His visitors had gone. He headed for the scotch bottle. His wife had told me earlier that he had had one drink earlier in the day and that that was enough. I had always been awed in his presence and would not have had the temerity to tell him not to have another drink.

When he had collected himself, he said, with a mixture of pride and sadness, that the men who had just left were emissaries of William O'Dwyer, who was then the mayor of New York. O'Dwyer had decided that it was time for New York to have its first black state supreme court justice and had selected Judge Watson for that honor.

This promotion made sense to me, and I immediately concluded that the judge's tears were those of joy. I was wrong. He said, with great sadness, that he did not have the money necessary to get the nomination for the post. Nomination as Democrat was a virtual assurance of election to a fourteen-year term. But, he said, he had no such funds. He added that he had four children to educate. Apparently, his night visitors had been brokers. Later, the judge told me that when O'Dwyer was told that Watson did not have the money, he said the offer should be made to another black lawyer. The lawyer mentioned was then a member of the state legislature. But, if any black lawyer at that time had easy access to the kind of money demanded, it was one of Harlem's best-guarded secrets. O'Dwyer was told that his second choice did not have the money either. As Judge Watson told me, Mayor O'Dwyer then said, "Oh, hell, give it to the other guy. At least he's a Catholic." Other versions have it that Cardinal Spellman had urged the nomination of the lawyer because he was a Catholic.

After that story became known, it was whispered as a joke that many Harlem lawyers who longed for political preference and judgeships were taking instructions to become Catholics. At that time Irish politicians still held sway in the city. It is a compliment to the black lawyers of Harlem and the strength of whatever religious faith they held that they did not immediately rush to become converts to Catholicism in the hope of gaining political blessings.

Scandals occasionally arise concerning the selection of judges because, it is rumored, the positions are bought. In 1930, George F. Ewald, a city magistrate, was charged with paying Tammany Hall $10,000 for his position. Politicians were said to be in control of appointments to the lower courts, and magistrates, once on the bench, were expected to pay off their district leaders again and again.

Corrupt magistrates did not fare well in the 1930s. The first woman judge in the history of New York, Jean H. Norris, was removed from the bench; three others resigned, and one fled the state as a result of politico-judicial corruption revealed by the Seabury Investigation.

Charles C. Burlingham, a former president of the Association of the Bar of the City of New York, published an article in *The New York Times* explaining how judgeships were bought. This period was the heyday of Tammany Hall, and its powers arranged the slates of names for which the city's electorate was to vote.

For years, the political pretension known as the "balanced ticket" existed, generally meaning a Catholic, a Jew, and a Protestant all, white. Seldom did it mean a Christian, a Jew and a black or Puerto Rican. For nominations to certain levels of the judiciary, no candidate was black or there was a strict quota of one. Each year, for example, Harlem's district leaders are allowed to dispute which single black (generally, a judge already sitting in a lower court) will be advanced to the state supreme court. In some years there is no black candidate for either the supreme or civil court in Manhattan.

After Edward Koch became Mayor of New York, he was occasionally challenged because of his failure to appoint blacks to the bench, especially the Criminal Court. The journalist, Jimmy Breslin commenting on the mayor's judicial appointments, titled a *Daily News* column "Color Them White."

Mayor Koch tends to brand all black lawyers as unfit. He piously says, with a straight face, that he makes appointments only on the basis of merit. Most of his appointments of blacks before 1986 were reappointments of sitting judges whose terms had expired, and whose judicial conduct had been low profile, and whose public remarks, if any, had not offended his ego. In his independent appointments he has usually ignored the recommendations of black politicians. One such appointment was the wife of his former parks commissioner, a woman never known to have practiced law in New York or to be identified with the black community of the city. Beginning in 1986, Koch appointed two young black women to Criminal Court. No other mayor had ever appointed two black women at the same time and Mary Johnson Lowe had, before that, been the only black woman ever to sit on that court.

As mentioned earlier, there was a time in New York when most of the commissioners and judges appeared to be the Irish beneficiaries of Tammany Hall. Almost imperceptibly during the late 1940s and the 1950s, the ethnic makeup of the bench began to change. There were more and more Jewish judges, and then the Italians seemed to realize that their numbers made them a powerful voting force in the city. The bench began to see more and more judges of Italian ancestry, as well as Italian-American police officers, both in the ranks and as executives of the Patrolmen's Benevolent Association.

Alas, the blacks and Hispanics continue to avoid the polls as though the ballot is a loathesome disease. The lack of a powerful voting bloc to make demands upon a mayor means that black commissioners and judges remain a slim census. In a 1971–1972 study of black judges undertaken by *Judicature*, the publication of the American Judicature Society, the paucity of black judges throughout the entire country was discussed. The optimistic assumption was expressed that those "primarily responsible for making the legal system function—e.g., lawyers, judges—represent a valid cross-section of all people. Yet, this is not the case."

In 1972, there were some 475 federal judges in America. Only 31 were black. Of 21,294 judges canvassed, only 255 were black. Today, the number of black judges in America is said to be no more than 500, an average of 10 in each of the fifty states. In such places as Alabama, Mississippi, Wyoming, or Idaho, the black judge is rare. In New York, there are some 3,500 judges, of which no more than 80 are black.

Because whites control the political system in New York, black judges are the arbitrary and capricious product of white politics. Now and then, despite the existence of black political district leaders and even though Raymond Jones, a black politician, was once the head of the Democratic County Committee in Manhattan, the posture of the white as ultimate boss is dramatically demonstrated.

For many years in New York, each black lawyer had hoped to be the one appointed to a seat on the federal bench. In the 1930s and 1940s, most of the black lawyers in New York were male. Only when the NAACP began to employ female lawyers did the public become aware that black women were practitioners. They served the NAACP well during the hazardous work in the South. Because they were not burdened by the mythological black penis, they were less likely to be lynched or run out of southern towns, where many cases had to be tried. White society has always seemed somewhat kinder to the black female and less fearful than it is of the black male.

Although white gossip has given to black women an aura of exotic sexuality, they have never been seen as a threat or danger to the system, as in the specter of rape. Because of slavery's tradition of the black mammy, black women are seen as the mother of us all, the first guardian, the national breast, the historical weaner, the symbol of dark affection for white infants, a trusty in America's vast prison of black captives. They were not regarded as revolutionaries. Although Harriet Tubman was a conductor on the underground railroad and a Union spy, and Sojourner Truth was an ardent abolitionist, neither was an insurrectionist, lusting for white blood, as did Denmark Vesey and Nat Turner.

Thus it was no surprise to anyone but those blind to history and its inevitable consequences when the white establishment decided that New York was ready for its first black federal judge and selected Constance Baker Motley as its choice. On the basis of professional excellence, the choice could not have been better. But also there was no better way for white society to show its contempt for black male lawyers. It was, in effect, a dramatic exhibition of the old-mammy theory, given a modern touch. This criticism should not be mistaken for a lack of chivalry, or a futile clinging to abrasive chauvinism. It is merely a comment on the ways of white society in making it clear to black males that they are at liberty but not free and, at best, on parole.

In 1978, at a Florida convention of the black National Bar Association, Judge Motley revealed herself as a keen and mistaken politician. Having once won the favor of the power brokers and having fully justified their daring, she sought to curry another blessing from the same source.

There was a vacancy on the U.S. Court of Appeals for the Second Circuit, based in New York. That court has been described as second in national prestige only to the U.S. Supreme Court. She obviously wanted that seat, and her qualifications are beyond dispute. It was rumored that the presidential appointment might be hers. Her speech to the women's division of the association was directed toward those whose promotional philanthropy she sought. She stirred her dozing audience by saying, without a wince of guilt, that in twenty-five years no trace of racial or color discrimination would remain in America. The applause was politely cynical, delivered at the point she paused to invite it.

Nevertheless, Judge Motley was passed over. The establishment had discovered a new black darling, a more youthful mother image, in Amalya Kearse, the only known black female partner in a Wall Street law firm, Hughes, Hubbard & Reed. Hardly anyone knew how to pronounce her name.

Black politicians were miffed because they were not consulted, and their vexation was intensified because Kearse was as remote from local politics as a Trappist monk. She had no known roots in New York, other than her employment. She was from New Jersey and had been educated at the University of Michigan Law School. A woman of noteworthy intellect, she had taught evidence at the New York University Law School and was a bridge expert of international stature. She became the first woman, black or white, to sit on the revered U.S. Court of Appeals.

Kathy Douglas, the young widow of Justice William O. Douglas and herself a lawyer, often made public speeches in a campaign to recruit women as law students. In an effort to attract both white and black women, she would say, "The law has long been too pale and too male." Lawyers in New York who are black and male might be expected to have little sympathy for the last half of that remark. But that same power that could make Mrs. Motley a judge could keep her where she was, despite her superior qualifications, which could match those of any candidate, no matter the color or sex.

***

My persistent concern has long been the white judges who, in large numbers, are called upon daily to preside over the trials of black defendants accused of crime. Are they qualified for such sociological tasks, only incidentally mixed with law? If so, how is

their competence defined? Is it the survival in them of a plantation concept of social divisions in life? What do they study in
college or law school that qualify them to decide the doom or
liberty of strangers to their neighborhoods, aliens to their way of
life, foreigners and outsiders to their clubs, their churches, their
synagogues, their history, their work, their culture, and their
folkways? What magic abolishes color in their eyes and gives
them instant objectivity and a license to analyze human foibles
entirely divorced from historical racism? How, indeed, does one
annul one's heritage and that of one's forefathers in this land or
the land from which one or both sides of the family came?

Do white judges ever consider why there are so many black
defendants in criminal causes? Do white judges ever wonder
why so few black lawyers appear before them? Do they ever inquire about the history of bar associations that used to exclude
Jews and blacks? Do they ever wonder, aloud or otherwise, why
there are so few black judges?

Whenever I have raised the subject of bar association discrimination against blacks, my white colleagues have professed never
to have noticed.

4

Bucking the System

There is a sociology of black citizens that is as unknown to white thought as are the strange complications of Sanskrit to English-speaking hearers. The slaveowning mentality of American whites is such that the proper "place" of blacks is never far from the thoughts of most of them.

In thousands of small and large ways, the demeaned "place" in society is part of America's daily drama. It is as though being black is a crime in itself and that those who are black chose the color of their skins after deliberate premeditation before being born.

This idea is no less ridiculous than blaming a black for his own lynching and accusing him of being black so that that event was certain to occur. The American dilemma is really no dilemma at all. It is the paradox of a national obstinance, fostered, treasured, codified, and carefully managed. The dilemma, in fact, is the white problem and no less a dilemma than a counterfeit paradox of constitutional libertarianism never intended to serve blacks at all.

Many whites who become judges, both in New York and in other parts of America, have been reared in a poisonous atmosphere. Racist emotions have been a polluting fallout, tainting those with a white skin, giving generation upon generation a continuing confirmation of the religion of the white skin's entitlement to privilege. The caste system has come to seem one of America's proprieties. Blacks with a well-expressed intelligence quotient are thought of as freaks, and, in a manner of speaking, it may be supposed that they are because they have survived without those mental defects that warrant confinement. Insults to the black persona, official and unofficial, are daily accumulations, as though to serve as reminders of history-as-a-threat.

Although respectable and conservative whites have organized charitable projects to welcome Vietnamese orphans and other survivors of America's lost cause in the Orient, African refugees from the residue and ravages of colonialism have never been the beneficiaries of any relocation undertaking. American immigration laws still favor those lands that produce blond, blue-eyed seekers of opportunity and severely limit the dark-skinned who strive for admission to this country.

There appears to be a fostered belief that blacks have a higher tolerance for pain than whites and are more peacefully stoical about deprivation. True it is that rude hardships have become the norm, and it seems that the tolerance of blacks for suffering in America is exceeded only by their unswerving allegiance to the country as a place to live and die.

Presumably, my former colleagues on the Criminal Court, especially those of my own age group, have been affected by two-toned Americanism. Some of them, when pressed about their pre-1960s visits to Florida, would profess not to have been aware of the racism that sent blacks to the back of the bus or Jim-Crowed them in the trains that traveled through the South, or barred them from restaurants, public parks, libraries, and universities.

Such ignorance alone should have barred them from high office.

One Criminal Court judge once asked me why I never ate lunch in the judges' lunchroom and remained aloof. Thereafter, he invited me to lunch at a nearby restaurant and made obvious efforts to win my confidence, suggesting that our families exchange visits, have dinner, and perhaps take a trip together. It was almost as though I had become the personification of Africa and he a pious missionary, bringing enlightenment to the heathen.

I used him as the KGB might use an espionage agent. He became my personal and secret investigator, my eyes and ears focused on my fellow judges. I referred to him as "99," after the Don Adams TV impersonation of a bungling spy. I relied on him to tell me what white judges talked about at their lunch meetings when no black was present, in their moments of relaxation, and in their casual conversations. The reports were hilarious, although presented earnestly and with a straight face. They revealed a pathetic ignorance and, now and then, an incredible illiteracy.

I was surprised to learn how many judges suspected that I was engaged in subversive and hate-filled plots to start a middle-east riot, to flee America, to seek instant citizenship elsewhere, and to elope with a white woman.

I was amused to learn that it was thought that all Negroes smoke Chesterfields. I had thought that, with the flooding of the cigarette market with new low-tar claims, the old brand names had been swallowed up forever. I think Judge Andrew R. Tyler would have been amazed to learn that, in New York City, he was regarded as the fearless leader of all blacks. He, incidentally, smokes only a pipe.

Jawn Sandifer was, understandably, their most lightly regarded subject. A low-profile Negro, officious and undistinguished, he had come to the bench through his allegiance to those in political power. He seemed a perfect example of how to win friends and influence people. After he passed the New York State bar examination, his work with the NAACP had made him acceptable as something of a civil libertarian. The truth is that he prospered through the NAACP both socially and commercially. Although there is certainly nothing exceptional with such exploitation, its significance in promoting the historical mission of the country's oldest civil rights movement is less clear. At one point, after becoming a judge, he was in charge of fair employment practices in the city's court system. Black and Hispanic court officers protested that during his tenure they were not promoted and that none were hired. It was not surprising that Sandifer's elevation inspired him to move from a comfortable section of Harlem. He appeased his judicial eminence by fleeing from the black neighbors who had been his clients to take up residence on Central Park West.

Among white judges, Edward Dudley is known as the system's favorite black son. His promotions on the judicial totem pole have been unmatched by those of any other black judge, except, possibly, Herbert Evans and with less reason. He was a perfect example of the Peter Principle. Ineffective as Administrative Judge of the City's Criminal Court, he was made Administrator of the Civil Branch of the State Supreme Court and a member of its Appellate Term. Within New York's jurisdiction he became the male Constance Baker Motley, but without her intellectual gifts. He also had been plucked from the legal staff of the NAACP for adoption by those in a position to make black judges.

I was known among the judges as one who was "crazy" and who deliberately opposed the system. I thus forfeited opportunities reserved for those blacks who knew their quiet place and kept it. Gossip had it that I could easily be promoted if I would only remember my "place" and stop making critical statements

92

about the judicial system and accusing it of being racist. Neither was I supposed to attack the police, many of whom appeared before me every day. It seemed that I was supposed to express gratitude for my position, not be cheeky, and, of course, not indulge in public expressions about the defects in the criminal justice system.

Some of my white colleagues suggested that I hated all white people and that my public remarks proved it. In short, it seemed that I was being chastised for not fully appreciating white condescension and polite contempt.

A white judge with whom I served on the Criminal Court, Joel Tyler, is now a federal magistrate. One morning, he stopped me in a public corridor of the courthouse and literally screamed, "You almost ran me down at Canal Street and Broadway!" I thought for a moment that he was unveiling a previously unseen sense of humor. But he immediately removed all basis for that supposition by continuing, in a loud voice and unmistakable heat, "And the only reason you did it is because I am white."

His mood appeared to be the product of a deep-seated chagrin and I sought to appease it by assuring him that, had I been certain that he was white, I would not have missed. I promised him that I would practice my aim on some worthier whites and get back to him in due course.

This response resulted in a description of me as "one black man who hates the guts of all whites," as my spy informed me. But because I had a white and affectionately devoted mother, I could smile at such declarative analyses of my tastes in skin colors.

The courthouse walls at 100 Centre Street serve as background scenery for the emotional atmosphere that troubles philosophical concepts of justice. Facing the public entrances to the building are concrete engravings of utterances that should have been great and wise. But as I mentioned earlier they are the words of slaveowning Thomas Jefferson, and they seem sullied by pomp and fatuity.

The public conduct of Thomas Jefferson has always emerged, for me, as historical posturing, by reason of his deeply held religious convictions, contrasted with his views of Negroes and his holding of them in bondage. Historians have done their faithful bit to apotheosize his life, even as they have for Washington. Apologias for slaveowning Christians punctuate the writings about the Founding Fathers, who managed the theft of this country from the Indians. Therefore, the quotations from Jefferson, the official handwriting on the walls of the courthouse, have an extremely hollow ring to some, especially when they speak of the administration of justice. Very few historians have explored the long-lasting relationship between Jefferson and black Sally Hemings. Only recently have blacks had an opportunity to become familiar with some of the more intimate details of that liaison.

All of us who profess to admire pure reason scoff at seers, witch doctors, and interpreters of tea leaves. Yet we live by fictions. Even so theoretically objective a discipline as the law thrives on unreality. An entire body of law is known as legal fictions. For example, we are allowed to annul marriages that have produced children. The annulment permits the parties to say they were never married, although the children remain legitimate and bear the name of the father.

History is no exception to the rule of fictions, as is demonstrated by certain facts about the Father of America. Only recently have we learned that, at the same time he was conducting revolution and rebellion against England, he was satisfying vanity by purchasing accessories from London.

Early childhood instruction is permitted to cover the warts and foibles of the hero because their revelation might make him human and nonheroic. There are some things, however, about the Criminal Courts Building, with its children's building-block lines and its infamy as the home of the Tombs, that smack of basic, hard-line truth. They are not fictions. They reflect the ethos not only of New York City but of the Christian prejudices of the nation.

If the country can be said to have a definable character, it may be found in the scribbled graffiti that leaps out at us from surprising places. The livid messages on the walls inside the various stairwells remained undisturbed for years. As though holy writ, one stark legend greeted all who descended the stairs from the fourth floor, appropriately enough, at the building's southern end. The words seemed like an aberrant prophecy. Their advice was: "Kill, kill, kill, but kill the niggers, Jews and spics first!" At last, the blacks had made it to first place in America, and the winning was to be their loss. We had become Nazi America's black Jews; we were the ingredients of what makes apartheid work, and in the halls of justice at that.

What is astonishing is not that the words were so carefully placed on the wall in large letters but that in a courthouse where a large proportion of blacks and Hispanics were supplicants for that elusive wraith, justice, those offensive words remained for so long a time. Neither blacks who came that way nor others who could not escape the proclamation calling for the death of so many human beings sought to cross out a single syllable.

In addition, there were writings beneath the words, such as "Right on!" and "Let's do it now!" In a city of graffiti and countergraffiti, the permanence of the insult reflected its tenacious adoption. A certain quality of American anti-Semitism was also revealed by the inscriptions on sidewalks and lamp posts, which said, "Jews for Jesus." The most constant subscript added to that legend was "Who Needs Them?" Others, like the one prevalent in Harlem saying, "Become Catholic," often had written beneath that advice, "Why?"

Why, too, were there no quotations from John Brown, Nat

Turner, Denmark Vesey, or William Wells Brown? Had the blacks unconsciously adopted the death wish expressed for them? It seemed that Ralph Ellison was right in saying that each black is an invisible man when it comes to the benefits of democracy.

One of the reasons why I have identified so closely with the struggles of the Jews is because they have had to endure oppressions in America that may be possessed of a stronger and more bitter animus than that reserved for blacks.

It was not difficult to notice, from time to time, that in addition to the Jewish aid given to the black civil rights movement, the Jews had their own causes to espouse at the same time. After World War II, when the United Nations began to flourish in the United States, Russia, with England, France and America, became one of the Big Four. Many Russians emigrated to America and especially to New York. They brought many stories of Jewish persecution in the Soviet Union. By the early 1970s a radical youth movement known as the Jewish Defense League (JDL) had become prominent. One of the causes to which it was dedicated was pointing up and publicizing what the Soviet Union was doing to its Jewish citizens, especially those who sought to emigrate to Israel. Often the JDL's conduct took the form of picketing and other demonstrations against the Russians accredited to the United Nations.

The JDL never hesitated to show the distaste of its members toward Soviet diplomats. Some of them were accused of daubing or splashing red paint on the buildings occupied by Moscow's representatives, some even of discharging a rifle in the direction of the Russian residence. Several of those cases had come before my bench.

The slogan of the youthful Jewish militants was "Never Again!" I understood its adamant sentiment perfectly. Such a brave and hopeful cry should have been usurped by the NAACP because blacks had been slaves. Obviously, the league was not deluded into thinking that "it can't happen here." They remembered the fate of the millions of Jews in Europe who thought that the Holocaust could not happen there. Such thoughts, as history has revealed, were little more than a bleak placebo.

Young Jews appear to believe that it makes better sense to come out fighting. They are as aware as I am of the latent and often overt anti-Semitism in America and the rest of the world. As recently as April, 1986, *The New York Times* reported from Dusseldorf that its mayor spoke of killing "a few rich Jews" to balance the city's budget.

The local Jewish organization, obviously respectable and without the JDL's passion, urged the dropping of charges against the mayor after he donated $41,000 to a children's cancer hospital. He doubtless claimed a substantial tax benefit. The JDL knows that discrimination must be fought without letup. They know, as I do, that prejudice must be publicly attacked by all who oppose it, even and *especially* if one is a judge.

I hope I have exerted some of the same angry passions as those that energize the Jewish Defense League. The last will and testament of Frederick Douglass bequeathed to all blacks the admonition, "Agitate, agitate, agitate."

The purpose of the Jewish agitation is in the cause of not *permitting* any further national atrocities to promote a Nazi-like Final Solution. The purpose of black agitation should be in the cause of not *permitting* the Christian morality of American democracy to sink, once again, into holding blacks in bondage, and to work to heal America of its racism.

Whenever prosecutions of Jewish Defense League members came before me, I always felt a keen sense of identification with the necessity to struggle and to agitate. After all, it seemed to me, the JDL's members were often treated as white niggers. To respectable and wealthy Jews, the league was a source of embarrassment, just as the conduct of black radicals seems to embarrass those blacks who believe themselves to be members of the bourgeoisie elite, or Afro-Saxons.

In one JDL case, the testimony revealed that some young Jewish men, passing the West 14th Street armory, noticed a piece of graffiti, not uncommon on walls and sidewalks of New York. Magic Marker capitals said, "Jew Go Home." The authors were doubtless the same ilk as those who would not wish to recognize the right of Israel to exist. The men stopped. One rang the armory bell. Someone peeked at him through an aperture in the door and demanded to know his mission. He stated his purpose, asking that the offending words be removed. He said that the man behind the door sneered and suggested, with an epithet, that the JDL member follow the advice offered by the protested legend.

He returned to his friends. They purchased some spray paint approximately the same color as the facade of the armory's tan. They returned and covered the graffiti. They were arrested and in due course came before me, charged with criminal mischief that diminished the value of the property. But, as one witness put it, the same armory authorities had quickly obliterated earlier graffiti that said, "Avenge Attica"; he said he felt if that writing could be removed, so too could the affront to the Jewish community.

After hearing the testimony, I ruled from the bench that the young defendants had not diminished the value of the armory but had improved the building by their act. The charges were dismissed, and the men were acquitted.

I was so impressed by what I regarded as commendable zeal and a proper revolutionary spirit on the part of the defendants that I sought their aid and expertise in painting out the "Kill, kill, kill" inscription, which lashed together as Final Solution victims blacks, Jews, and Hispanics. I had long ago asked the building custodian to erase the writing before some aberrant patriot became so impressed that he undertook single-handedly to begin instant executions. I was told, however, in the robot fashion of civil service inflexibility, that painting in the building was done only on a schedule and that particular area was not due for another year or so.

In a plot that could have ruined my judicial career, I arranged for my newly discovered allies to come to my chambers on the next weekend, where I would provide the paint for the obliteration of the murderous advice. But the jeopardy of a criminal mischief charge and the disgrace of being formally unfrocked were avoided at the last moment. When five young men arrived at the appointed hour, we proceeded with paint and brush to the guilty stairwell, only to discover that the wall had been newly painted, and officially so, for "wet pain" signs were neatly posted.

Shortly thereafter, some JDL members were brought before my court, charged with jumping bail for an alleged earlier offense, they had been scheduled to go on trial three days from the time they were faced by the new charges. It seems that they were arrested at Kennedy Airport while on board an El Al plane, headed for Israel. They had one-way tickets. The circumstances of how the arrest came about were not stated.

I suggested to the assistant district attorney that the charges might have to be dismissed because no one could be accused of jumping bail until it was shown that he did not appear on a date when he was scheduled to be present in court. Three days remained before the JDL members were due in court on the prior charges. I granted a short recess to the prosecutor to consider my analysis.

At that point, the system's wrath reached out to demonstrate emphatically whose power was orchestrating justice. I was impressed with the minor and minority role played by judges, and in particular myself. The late Frank Hogan, New York's celebrated district attorney for more than three decades, was the beneficiary of a public relations coup. He enjoyed a national image as an angel of justice. He was nearly deified for his alleged impeccable propriety in running the country's busiest prosecutor's office. It was said that his was the one office that was wholly divorced from politics and that only merit characterized his selection of young assistants.

I had a different view of his reputation. He had once been in my chambers on a strange and unannounced mission. His chief of the Criminal Courts Bureau was with him and was allowed to interrupt me at lunch at my desk by telling me, "Judge, we just want you to know that the D.A.'s office does not approve of anything you do. We read everything you write, with the intention of appealing to a higher court." That was in 1972, when I was still a judicial neophyte. I was stunned by what I regarded as a threat to my independence and an effort to deter me.

The impudence of such a visit was doubtless inspired by the protective cloak of the Hogan mythology. Somehow, he had managed to create in the public mind, and in the minds of politicians, that he was an indispensable man of justice. I suggested that he seemed to be exhibiting the political power of his so-called nonpolitical reputation, and I urged that his approval or disapproval of a judge's conduct be expressed elsewhere and in a manner less likely to be regarded as an effort to tamper with a judge's exercise of discretion. I stated, as well, that the impromptu conference was unnecessary.

If a judge strayed into error or violated judicial canons, onerous proceedings were available to attempt to unfrock or remove the judge. As the audacity of the invasion of my chambers became more apparent, I ended the audience with what I trusted was obvious curtness and resumed eating my lunch and reading my newspaper. I could not imagine a district attorney or one of his emissaries confronting a white judge in such a manner.

At the end of the recess in the JDL case then before me, the assistant district attorney sought to amend the charging information by making the offense attempted bail-jumping. The possibilities of such a charge were fraught with the speculative happenstance of mind-reading, and I offered the view that it, too, would have to be dismissed. I added further vexation to the prosecutor by noting that, with today's supersonic planes, there could be no presumption that the young men could not return from Israel in time to keep their court appointments in New York.

Suddenly there was an anxious conference away from the bench. I continued with other court business. Hogan's office was busy with the Administrative Judge, who dictated the assignments of the Criminal Court judges, saying where they would sit and for what period. The whisper was that I had prejudged the case and that the needs of justice required that the case be reassigned to a different judge. This was odd because I had presumed the innocence of the young defendants, an ethic I had always thought constitutional.

Shortly thereafter, one of the court clerks advised me that the case had been assigned to another judge and that I had been disqualified from ever handling any other Jewish Defense League cases. The matter was transferred to Judge Milton Samorodin, who was known as a strict and severe conservative. The Legal Aid Society resented his exhibitions of hostility both toward them and their poor minority clients. They uncharitably referred to him by a name I am not at liberty to print here.

Most judges, as might be expected, are the by-products of politics, in one way or another. Whether judges pay for their appointments to the bench has long been the subject of speculation. There have been many investigations through the years in efforts to uncover evidence of such corruption. I have been asked many times how much I paid for my appointment. I was told by one black lawyer that he had been expecting to get the appointment I received, and he asked me pointedly how much I paid to win preference over him. I was more amused than angered by such unflattering questions. The facts of my appointment by Mayor John V. Lindsay perhaps differ from the usual political appointments, as I have mentioned.

In March 1971, about one year after my appointment, *Life* magazine carried an article entitled "I Have Nothing to Do with Justice." It was the text of a long interview with Martin Erdmann, who was then the chief trial counsel for the Legal Aid Society. He was quoted as having said:

> There are so few trial judges who just judge, who rule on questions of law and leave guilt or innocence to the jury. And Appellate Division judges aren't any better. They're the whores who become madams. I would like to [be a judge] just to see if I could be the kind of judge I think a judge should be. But the only way you can get it is to be in politics or buy it and I don't even know the going price.

Such cynical observations moved the Appellate Division justices to prefer charges against Erdmann. After long and expensive litigation, the court of appeals finally dismissed the charges, though taking the opportunity to voice disapproval of Erdmann's "taste, civility, morality or ethics." Two judges thought Erdmann should have been censured for his remarks.

It would have been interesting to know Erdmann's feelings about judges as whores and madams and his thoughts about buying judgeships. After he became a judge of the Criminal Court of New York City himself, he could be expected to harbor at least one critical metaphor concerning the system of criminal justice and its judges.

Most judges seem to find the genesis of their position in their former political clubs. The ambitions of the clubhouse lawyer mandate certain base necessities. These urgencies do not vary as much between black and white political clubs as do the comparable rewards.

Lawyers, anxious to get profitable cases and attract their district leader's attention, must faithfully attend twice-weekly meetings and be generous in handing out free advice. Their doing so makes the club attractive, the leader a community resource, and results in mouth-to-mouth advertising for the selfless lawyers.

The leader's rewards are the prestige and reputed money he gets from his occasional distribution of benefactions. Because the quota of political appointments available to black district leaders is limited, there is avid competition for appointments. Such quotas involve judgeships as well as other nominations that, in a solidly Democratic area, are synonymous with election. The fealty paid to a district leader by lawyers of ambition and favor-seekers often makes sycophants of those who write their own obeisant scripts and roles.

An example, thought not to be isolated or unique, of how far obeisance to a district leader may go to appease his ego or anger is found in the conduct of one of my former law partners, who was an active politician.

In 1954, Herbert B. Evans and I practiced as partners in the same law firm. After a career of political appointments he became the Chief Administrative Judge for the State of New York, under the supervisory guidance of the Chief Judge of the Court of Appeals.

When Averell Harriman ran for governor in 1955, Evans did volunteer work for a group of wealthy citizens working through the political club in Harlem of which he was a member. When Harriman won, the people with whom Evans had worked recommended that Evans be given a role as an assistant counsel to the new governor. Evans thus became the first black to occupy such an important office when Harriman conferred that favor.

Evans's district leader in Harlem was furious because a member of his fiefdom had gone outside his power base to win a reward. Learning of his fearless leader's ire, Evans immediately sought to repair the damage.

He appeared at the next meeting of his club. In the guise of a sinner making public atonement through confession, he announced to the gathering that he wished to thank his leader for having interceded to make possible his appointment by the governor. He thereby appeased the leader's sense of propriety and local hegemony and also reaffirmed the leader's fictitious statewide power. Both knew that the leader had nothing to do with Evans's appointment. Later, Evans became a justice of the appellate division of the supreme court. His elevation at various times is interesting because his merit is beyond dispute. As of this writing he is the first and only black partner in the Shea Gould firm.

Evans was always an extremely careful person. Because he and his wife had no children, he was able to devote one room of his Manhattan apartment to express his intellectual tastes. At the entrance to the apartment, there was a table on which was prominently displayed a book of philosophy. It symbolized Evans's desire to create an impression he believed to be serviceable. In such great affection did he hold his self-image that after he and his first wife divorced, he effected a reconciliation with her before seeking public office.

Both white and black judges are energized by political necessities in seeking what they believe to be the godly power of the black robe. Although there is no known formal college education to fit one for success in a political club, most club members who head for careers in the law do take certain prescribed courses that are thought to be helpful in preparing for law school.

Presumably lawyers who reach the bench have studied the political sciences, some business courses, white history, economics, and accounting. Few, however, have touched the heart of social work and the degraded society from which most criminal defendants come.

Few white judges have black friends with whom they have

shared intimate life experiences on the basis of close knowledge and affectionate regard and egalitarian esteem. The whites who become judges of the Criminal Court are all too often graduates of schools and colleges that teach the history of America within the boundaries of the usual heedless clichés of bare dates and occurrences.

Whenever I have mentioned that Alexander Hamilton was said to have had a mother who was one-eighth Negro and was born on the West Indian island of Nevis, white judges have seemed astonished and unbelieving, as though I had invented an instant and fictitious biography.

Consternation is intensified when I mention that Hamilton's mother had a long and lasting marriage with a man named Levine, and that his father remains such a shadowy figure that there has been some speculation that Hamilton himself was either a Levine or part Negro. I then offer the opinion that Hamilton, a handsome Founding Father, was never elected president because he was believed to be either Negro or Jewish, and those who have been bred on the romantic obscurantism of American history appear to be aghast. Of course, Hamilton could not have been president in any event since he was born outside the United States. It is not generally known that Hamilton's application for admission to Princeton University in the 1700s was rejected on the basis of racial consideration.

Following the showing of Alex Haley's *Roots* to a national television audience, I was asked by a white judge what I thought about the excitement generated by the program. I said that it was about time white citizens were exposed to a historical past that had been a virtual secret to them. Perhaps, I said, whites could now get some vague idea of what it meant to be black in America and what a great miracle black survival had been.

The judge replied that he thought the show was outrageously biased because it failed to show one "good" slaveowner. He could see no contradiction in the use of the term "good" in conjunction with the moral corruption of slavery, a condition that made the Constitution a fraud to blacks.

Unable to comprehend opposition of terms, he could not, of course, understand why he thought that blacks should have a special "place" in American society or that the American sociology of slavery had any impact on both black and white life of today. Neither could he see anything but genetic humor in the white joke that Alex Haley adopted, thus reducing *Roots* to speculative imagination and a meaningless and maudlin display. The black world seems closed off from the white one. Whites seem to know less about blacks than blacks know about them.

Black education in America, with its segregated inequality, has always been neglected. Now that public schools in many cities are predominantly black, the standards of segregation remain the norm. It is astonishing, in a nation with so many colleges and universities that few people realized the abrasive debt that slavery and its consequences would inflict on future generations, with financial, emotional, and moral burdens that will be borne by many generations yet to come.

With all of the passion and ritual Americans reserve for religion, it should not be stunning to discover in the country's ethos an incurable anti-intellectual turbulence. The hundreds of people who lined up before the United States Supreme Court the night before the *Bakke* case was to be argued were not there so much out of intellectual curiosity as to make certain, by their presence, that sacred American racial principles would not be destroyed.

My fellow judges in the Criminal Court could discuss the surface details of this latest Supreme Court ruling, as it came to them in precis form, but could grasp nothing of the sociolegal significance of black citizens having been compelled to do battle in the courts for the two hundred years of the nation's existence to win what whites routinely took for granted and certified in the saying, "free, white, and twenty-one."

Never having had to sue for the right to enter a public library, park, or swimming pool; never having attended a one-room shack masquerading as a schoolhouse; never having had to beg for the constitutional right to vote to spend money to eat in a restaurant, to seek refuge in a hotel or inn, it was impossible for them to have genuinely humane feelings about blacks as persons, as opposed to *black* persons.

None could see the analogy of black men begging for their manhood in white America. Their prejudice was built in and preshaped. They might never understand. The black endurance had been *their* experience. Hearing or reading about such constitutional travesties was the same to them as seeing a dull and pointless film dealing with unreal inventions. The everyday life and straitened posture of black existence and survival could never be felt by whites, even poor whites.

Robert F. Kennedy, whom blacks revered, sought advice from some black intellectuals when he ran for the Senate from New York. But he had no patience with Lorraine Hansberry when she remarked that there was no use expecting blacks to act like whites until they were treated like whites.

Because of such emotional and intellectual shortcomings, whites could both rejoice over and fear in the 1955 Supreme Court ruling that segregation in the public schools, based on race, was unconstitutional. Innocent optimists hailed the ruling as a giant step forward in human relations.

It was not.

What the Court said, in effect, was that although segregation was illegal, the South could nevertheless continue its racist policies until it was convenient for the Old Confederacy to make changes.

The due and deliberate speed mentioned by the Court became a national snail's pace, characterized by diversionary disputes over the role busing should or should not play in the purifying process. The decision itself, then, reeked of unconstitutionality because it upheld a constitutional affront.

So powerful were the tenured congressional leaders and so confident were they that they could overcome this paper challenge to their way of life that they announced to the world how they proposed to flaunt the ruling. They regarded it as a trespass on their white aristocracy, and they revived antebellum ghosts in an advertisement of arrogant white inhumanity. Old Sam Ervin, a self-styled country lawyer and former North Carolina judge, J. William Fulbright, and eighty-eight other southerners announced in Congress what they called their "Declaration of Constitutional Principles." This brazen attempt at usurpation of the Supreme's Court's mandate became known as "the Southern Manifesto."

The signers of that retrograde whimsy became reincarnated slaveowners. It was as though Simon Legree had come out of retirement to lead them into a modern plantation society of slaves and master. If proof were needed to confirm the estrangement of blacks and whites, it can be found in that manifesto.

Its leaders were all well-educated whites in positions of national power. They were not visibly poor-white malcontent members of the Ku Klux Klan. Fulbright was regarded as scholarly and an internationalist, and Senator Ervin, a lawgiver, lent prestige to the manifesto's authority. Sam Ervin was also a giver of copies of the Constitution to all who came to visit him in Washington. Apparently, his gift included the emancipatory amendments. His retirement from the Senate was regarded with relief by blacks.

The scandal of the "Southern Manifesto" was not known to have inspired outraged objections by white judges. Their silence could only be interpreted as tacit approval. The mute posture of black judges was a separate-but-equal disgrace. This happened in 1956 but seemed to hark back to 1857 to Dred Scott and to the doctrine of his case, which said no Negro had any rights that any white man was bound to respect.

How could local judges in New York ever doubt that the proper treatment of black defendants in the criminal courts should find its origins in what our national leaders did? As judges, they would certainly not man the picket lines* in a show of insurgent disagreement with the manifesto's petulant exhibitionism. Instead of acting, they continued to react.

Judges always find it best not to be too controversial, and certainly it is in the best interests of their careers not to be thought to harbor controversial concerns—a strange phenomenon in a calling so fraught with disputation. Even with stalemates among the jurors, that very nondecision is the product of irreconcilable disagreement.

Most judges, then, have assigned themselves the role of Olympians, presiding over dispute but not engaging in it. This is doubtless one of the reasons for the slowness of the law to adopt changes. Enslavement to tradition is not always a sign of stability; all too often it symbolizes inertia. In most societies, the law is allowed to act as the manager of overt human conduct, deciding what is proper, what is improper, and what sanctions to impose for breaches of propriety. Any inflexible allegiance to the past for definitions of conduct would be a denial of change and of the reasoning that should enlighten the law.

Oliver Wendell Holmes, through his muscular dissents over three decades of service as United States Supreme Court justice, is generally regarded as a liberal by historians of the law. Yet

---

*In 1985 and 1986, some judges did depart from their usual habits and manned picket lines outside the South African Consul's office on Park Avenue, led by Robert Abrams, New York's Attorney General, who had his entire staff in the line on one of the coldest winter nights.

he attacked leftists for emotionally taking up the case of Sacco and Vanzetti.

Holmes wrote to his friend, Harold J. Laski, "A thousand-fold worse cases of Negroes came up from time to time, but the world does not worry over them."

Neither did Holmes waste much worry over blacks. Possibly this was because—although he was a critic of the sometimes dead hand of the past on progress—his concern was for more arcane matters than equality for black citizens.

Whites seem to follow a "rules-of-the-game" code of acceptance of other whites. It is as though life in America is an exclusively white club, and the members can do no wrong.

Courtly white gentlemen from the South, whose sworn duty appears to be appeasing the worst elements of rural and urban prejudice against black existence, have always been accorded great honor. They were experts in filibusters that had as their aim the Christian oppression of black skin.

Pious national leaders and their community churches could all unite in that essay of oppression known as the Southern Manifesto. They advertised their nation's rebuke to the Supreme Court for being so timid when it abandoned the claimed virtues of a slave society. These good Christians proclaimed the great danger to democracy from ignoring the historical propriety of the necessary "place" of the brutish black in American society.

That men of national repute could conduct themselves in such an inhumane manner, and without shame, was a tribute to their power and the tolerance of a country which, in honoring them, upheld contempt for blacks. These were men, in the main, who had always lived a Southern Manifesto even before one was formalized. They had come from sections of the country where the right of blacks to vote or to have a decent education had always been suppressed. Another Charles Sumner would be needed in the Congress to focus attention on the humanity of black citizens.

I mention these things to give some description of the emotional and racial ecology in which those who became judges in this country were allowed to thrive, to prosper, and to reap great honor. America's caste system, which made blacks a separate and untouchable group, has all too often received negative leadership even from the White House.

Franklin D. Roosevelt, long regarded by both blacks and Jews as the earthly savior the nation from the Great Depression and the fearless leader of the Allies, salvaging European civilization from the Nazis, was less than heroic in some ways. He emerges from the history of his time as an anti-Semite and a racist whose attitude toward blacks was one of abiding contempt. Blacks appear to worship Roosevelt so passionately because they believe that he single-handedly abolished the Depression.

Roosevelt presided over a phase of history of which I was a tiny part, that is, the racial segregation of American troops. The paradox of American soldiers, as separate and unequal victims of democracy's racism fighting to destroy Hitler's racism, seemed meaningless to Roosevelt.

The great military heroes who came back from Europe and the Pacific in triumph, Douglas MacArthur, Omar Bradley, George Marshall, Mark Clark, and Dwight D. Eisenhower, all testified before Congress that the integration of the armed forces would be disastrous to the morale of the white troops. Little thought was given to the morale of the black soldiers and sailors.

Many whites who served in the segregated forces and who accepted that arrangement as perfectly natural eventually became leaders at the bar and my colleagues on the bench. Their racial attitudes were products of a period when black naval personnel were restricted to the status of messmen, that is, floating domestics. When I asked them what they did during and before World War II to object to this racist travesty, they generally replied, "Nothing," and added, "After all, Bruce, it was national policy then."

They were wrong, of course. National policy is declared by the Constitution and its amendments. What they meant was that it was a national practice of raw racism and a heedless flaunting of the Constitution, which they supported by not protesting. It was, in short, their way of admitting that they accepted the racial dichotomy as normal. They did not say but may have suspected that any overt declaration against racism by whites often resulted in such whites being called communists and worse, thus endangering their careers. Blacks simply were not worth that peril.

And so they participated in the pageant that saw the mightiest fighting force in the world carefully divided into racial categories. Lawyers, young men who would become lawyers, and judges played an active and supportive role in American racism. They were indispensable parts of a national oppression. They were in the conservative mold of the typical American lawyer.

I never ceased to remind my white colleagues of the repressive influences that were allowed to shape their thinking on race and created so much social distance between them and all blacks, including those of educational and artistic standing. My words did not ingratiate me with the judges of my generation. Except for one or two white judges, my relationship with my fellow jurists was one of surface courtesies and an occasional exchange of greetings. I had no love for them and less respect.

Early in my career, I had protested to Judge James Leff that most of my colleagues did not speak to me. With characteristic bite and cynical insight, he said "It's a fringe benefit." Other than Arthur Blyn, for whom I have the highest respect and affectionate regard, I have never wished to chat with any of them. I consider most of them as an abject lot, religiously devoted to obedience to the dictates of court administration as a way of advancing their own promotion within what I regard as a Neanderthal system.

Although they might grumble quietly, they are obedient to the administrative infrastructure, knowing that steadfast allegiance will promote their careers and that criticism would accomplish the opposite.

Under our system, judges who dispose of the greatest number of cases in the shortest possible time are the ones most favored. Perhaps they are much wiser than I. They saw how I was treated. For them to avoid similar treatment was certainly not unreasonable.

Justice in such hands becomes a numbers game, in which questions of humanity are disposed of summarily. Put bluntly, success in the game meant disposing of as many black and Hispanic bodies as possible. This was done by exacting pleas of guilty or by conducting speedy trials.

Prosperity in such statistics wins one a promotion as an acting Supreme Court justice. That temporary glory results in an increase in pay and prestige, those indispensable symbols of American success. The increase in pay and prestige, not to mention power, served as powerful goads to comply with the system's rewards for such conduct.

Further inspiration was discovered in the possibility of a nomination to run for a fourteen-year term as a Supreme Court justice without the limiting qualification of the word "acting" before one's name. For the most part, a numbers game was ensured, and one's career was reduced to a batting-average statistic. Each month, a mimeographed sheet reported how many cases the judges had and how many had been disposed of, either by trial or by pleas of guilty. No similar reports revealed a judge's wisdom or how he had served the ends of justice.

The anxiety of my Criminal Court colleagues in avoiding any "trouble" with the administrative hierarchy, made them experts at glad-handing and back-slapping, as though the court were just another back room of their favorite political club. It was easy to become adept at ignoring the genuine issues that always troubled the court.

Early in 1971, there were constant bomb scares and at least one bomb exploded in the building. The two presiding justices of the First and Second Judicial Departments convened an emergency meeting of the Criminal Court judges to discuss what course to follow in the event of a catastrophe. The steps to be taken in the event of an explosion or even a rumor that a bomb had been hidden in the courthouse were outlined.

After speeches by the two presiding justices, praising the manner in which all court personnel had bravely carried on despite the dangers posed by radicals protesting the war in Vietnam, the floor was opened for questions from the assembled judges.

One judge, who had many years experience and was a member of a distinguished family, stood up and asked, "Is it true that we will have a four-day weekend for the Fourth of July?" Such a question reflects on what ranks as the most urgent concern of a judicial officer, as opposed to serious exploration of the humanitarian issues that are always raised by charges and the prosecution and defense of criminal trials.

The police have easy access to sympathetic media. The officers who work in the courts, call the calendars, and keep order are all ambitious to become *real* police officers. In the meantime, they carry prominently displayed weapons and are known as "peace officers." They have great affection for the policemen they like so much to imitate, and they act as spies for the PBA, reporting gossip they believe the police should know about certain judges.

The assistant district attorneys also eagerly call the press whenever they want negative publicity for a judge they do not like. With the police, the district attorneys and the court officers are "Bruce watchers." My slightest disagreement with the po-

114

lice was quickly reported to the newspapers and television stations. My most casual expression of criticism directed at the police becomes in the minds of the officers an indefensible indictment.

In a time of great criminal activity and public fear about safety in the streets, the police were extremely effective in polishing their own image as front-line guardians of the common weal. This was their way of exploiting fear and near hysteria in the city, as they sought to demonstrate that, despite their heroic efforts, the judges were undoing their brave labors. Few citizens questioned the effectiveness of New York's Finest or remembered the scandals or corruption that, from time to time, revealed a very human side of the police.

Hardly anyone deplored the resistance of the police to the periodic suggestions that they should live in the city they were sworn to protect twenty-four hours a day. In effect they justified their flight to the white suburbs, away from the object of their protection. The constant barrage of police propaganda has helped create a cynical mood among the public.

The canon of the criminal law that one is presumed innocent until proved guilty beyond a reasonable doubt seems now to be suspect. After the arrest of a suspect, few citizens are content to wait for a trial or the presentation of evidence. The hysteria and fear of the times call for immediate "justice" and this results in instant conviction in the public mind.

The police have seldom failed to emphasize their role as heroic bulwarks of salvation in a world of desperate criminal cruelty. And some of the police have been sturdy heroes indeed. Many of the young officers appear to take their calling seriously, and they devote a professional zeal to their work. Others have become cynical. Many of the latter are seen in courts during off-duty hours, sometimes both day and night, with those they have arrested.

Sitting around court waiting for an arraignment of their captives is one way of earning $15 per hour in overtime, and, all too often, many of the arrests seem to have been made only for the purpose of collecting the overtime pay.

To make an arrest look "serious," some officers will charge the defendant with a felony when they know that the charge is likely to be reduced at some point by the district attorney. And when charges are reduced, the officer can shake his head as though in wonderment that administrative villains can so callously undo his heroism. It is the expression of the officer's anger, whether real or feigned, that the television audience sees when an officer is interviewed.

In one case, in which a white defendant was charged with homicide, my analysis of the facts, as they were presented to me, indicated that the death of the victim was an accident following a flare-up between former friends. The deceased had been knocked down in a fist fight with his friend. He arose and walked away and died shortly thereafter.

I released the defendant without bail. He had no money. The next day, the headlines in the press and the reports on television made it appear that I had let loose on the unsuspecting community the most dangerous and depraved criminal ever to walk the streets. When the same homicide charge was dismissed by a white judge some weeks later, one could discover that fact only by searching fine print for an item so small it amounted to no more than a brief footnote.

The police had found in me the perfect foil and a judicial officer they could depict as a foe of law and order. This aided and abetted their own careers, making it appear that even the courts opposed the doing of a policeman's duty although the charge was prostitution. The *Daily News* hailed him as a latter-day messiah of morality as though that oppressive act had not only been correct but had also eliminated the second oldest profession once and for all. Knowingly or unwittingly, judges often fine prostitutes then parole them to earn the fine. Judges who do this are

116

known as "Johns," since it is to them that the illegal earnings are brought.

By 1972, I had become the focus of unceasing police ire. In one of his 1978 columns in the *Daily News*, Jimmy Breslin, commenting on one police attack directed to me, suggested that the police had selected me as their favorite target for two principal reasons.

One was that I had become a symbol to be exploited as an example of the grave difficulties with which they had to cope. And I was pictured as archetypical of a criminal justice system that ignored police valor and exhibited more sympathy for criminals than for the police. The result, of course, was to divert attention from the criminal conduct of the police themselves.

In addition, as Breslin said, there could be nothing better as a whipping *boy* than a black *man* in his fifties. The police were powerfully assisted in their advertisements by the fact that their pronouncements were generally accepted as little less than holy writ and *ex cathedra* bulls from an infallible lay Vatican. The term "Turn 'Em Loose Bruce," dramatized the contempt in which I was held by the police.

On the question of detaining defendants simply to keep them off the street and under arrest until they could be tried, few recalled that in 1970 the state legislature had specifically rejected any semblance of preventive detention in New York.

Preventive detention, of course, is wholly destructive of the traditional American presumption of innocence because it is based on the theory that pre-trial confinement prevents a defendant from "doing the same thing again." Police officers who are arrested and charged naturally believe passionately in pre-trial release on their own recognizance and in honoring the presumption of innocence.

One of the troubles with the Police Department is that, from its earliest days as a formal organization and until recently, it has been dominated by what has become to be known as the "Irish

117

Mafia." The Irish came to believe that the department belonged to them. It was their territorial imperative. They exhibited a spirit of protective ownership.

The failure of the potato crop in Ireland in 1846 and 1847 brought millions of Irish immigrants to America through the Port of New York. The subjugation of the Irish by the English dated back some two hundred years before the potato famine and had generated so powerful a hate among the Irish that many believed that the famine itself was an English abomination. Numerous pacification expeditions to Ireland by British forces and the presence of English policing that island have given the Irish an historical detestation for English authority.

At the time, so many were arriving in New York, one of the first sights greeting them on the streets was police officers dressed like English constables. Offended by such symbols of detested British authority, young bands of Irish bully boys adopted the habit of waylaying the officers and beating them. So vexed were the administrators of police authority that they sought to eliminate such beatings by allowing the officers to dress in mufti and wear only copper stars or shields of their authority. This resulted in insults being hurled at the officers by the young Irish street marauders, who called the officers "coppers." That term has since been shortened to "cop" and accepted, even by the police, as the name for an honorable profession.

Nevertheless, the police continued to be victims of the roaming and generally unemployed gangs and, finally, the administrators adopted a kind of reverse policy of "If they continue to beat us, let's join them." The Irish bully lads were adopted as police officers almost wholesale, without the intellectual impediment of a civil service examination. Policing became a virtual Irish monopoly in New York, and many other Irish immigrants came to America specifically to become police officers in the city.

Yet America's vaunted hospitality to immigrants was not always kind to the Irish. They were the poor of New York, along with the city's blacks. Indeed, the Irish were known as "white niggers," and they competed with the blacks for the lowest jobs available, one of which was emptying outhouses, primitive conveniences common in New York City before plumbing and sewage disposal became modernized.

As is all too often the case when the poor compete among themselves for the crumbs of society, the black and white poor came to hate each other, each seeing in the other minority some deprivation of themselves. So acute was the mutual detestation that, by the time of the Civil War, when a man eligible for military duty could purchase exemption by paying $300, the poor Irish (who were militarily white) could not afford that luxury.

In angry resentment both at their poverty and at the supposed cause of the war (the abolition of slavery), the young Irish rebelled against enlisting in the Union Army by parading through the streets of New York. They yelled that they were not going to fight to "free the niggers." They were otherwise disposed to fighting, however, for their hostile progress through the streets allowed them to beat Negroes and even burn down the Colored Orphan Home, along with any poor unfortunates who remained in that doomed building.

Thus was crystallized an ethnic tradition of dislike and suspicion directed at the blacks by the Irish, whose protective coloration and success as modern Americans give no clue of their disturbed past as victims of discriminations that rival those historically reserved for blacks.

The power of the Irish in modern New York society is such that, despite the recent prominence of Italians and others in the ranks of the Police Department, no mayor of New York, with two exceptions, has dared appoint any person as police commissioner who was not Irish Catholic. Theodore Roosevelt once

119

served as commissioner and Mayor Edward I. Koch appointed Benjamin Ward to that office as the first black commissioner.

It seems that the entire department has adopted a view of blacks which acts out the ancient observation that "the oppressed, when liberated, become the oppressors." That oppression is reflected in different ways, other than by the use of raw and brutal force against blacks and Hispanics. The force used, however, is just as deadly in its side effects.

For many years, blacks were not even considered as possible candidates for appointment to the force. It was not until 1911 that Manhattan saw its first black officer, and he remained a lonely quota of one for a long long time. An enormous man, Samuel Battle resembled Jack Johnson in stature, and this appearance of being able to live up to his name contributed largely to his survival in the private-club hostility of the department.

Anyone aware of the history of the Irish in New York believes that the hostility between the police and the blacks stems from the ancient competition between the two groups when both were regarded and treated as niggers of different colors. With their protective coloration, the Irish have so far progressed in American society that one no longer even hears the contemptuous mention that used to distinguish the "shanty" toughs from the "lace curtain" gentility among them.

It is not only the deadly violence of police brutality against blacks that illustrates the traditional antagonism. Now and then the police attitude is expressed in other ways. One illustration may be found in an incident that occurred in 1952. A black man, Billy Rowe, was walking along Park Avenue on his way to visit his friend, Ed Sullivan, the television personality. A white woman was walking just in front of him. Apparently, she got the impression, through vanity or otherwise, that Rowe was following her. She saw a police squad car and summoned the white officers to rescue her from the danger of her imagined pursuer.

An officer called out to Rowe, "Hey, you!" Rowe at first ignored the call. It came again. Looking at the officer evenly, Rowe replied, "If you wish to speak to me, I have a name." The officer then said, "Just a minute there, I'm a police officer." Rowe said, "Oh, are you? Well, then, I happen to be one of your bosses." He then exhibited his shield: he was at that time the first black deputy police commissioner in the country. The officers retreated in some embarrassment. The damsel in distress must have been puzzled by their sudden disappearance.

The national police organizations appeared at one time to have taken instructions from the racist persuasion of officers from the South—a time when lynchings of blacks seemed normal, especially when the police themselves were participants in such gory carnivals. Dr. David Musto, of Yale University, in his book *The American Disease,* cites the influence of racist myths and rumor in convincing policemen that not only were blacks addicted to the use of cocaine but that it made black skins virtually impervious to the .32 caliber bullet and that officers need .38 caliber weapons to shoot blacks.

That American police departments now have the .38 caliber weapon as their standard arm is a reflection of what a widely held racist view can accomplish. It was also thought that the Negro's fondness for cocaine stimulated his sexuality, thus making white women vulnerable to black rape.

This general fear of the Negro and the feeling of necessity for keeping him in his place was encouraged by such ethnic gossip and also included apocrypha that the Negro's marksmanship was sharpened and perfected by his use of cocaine. Coca-cola, which used to contain cocaine, was thought, for that reason, to be the favorite refreshment of America's Negro underclass.

The persuasive power of the police has not stopped at the press, which, understandably, might overdramatize cause and effect so as to aid and abet the sale of newspapers. Now and then, the courts and judges reveal an urgent necessity to ally themselves with police sentiment, even though the vocations of the police and the court are strikingly different.

In the Grutolla case, masses of police demonstrated in the courtroom their noisy disagreement with allowing the defendant to be at the qualified liberty represented by his ability to meet the low bail I had imposed. It was Christmas, went one argument, and while Officer Dowd lay in the hospital struggling to recover from a critical wound, he was deprived of the usual holiday celebrations with his wife and children. The press had also emphasized the police outcry that Grutolla was out in the streets, at liberty to do *again* what he had then only been accused of doing.

That all of the actors in the Grutolla incident were white did not remove the taint of racism. The attack on me had been so virulent that it practically linked my sympathies with criminals who shoot or slay police officers. Almost immediately after I reinstated the same bail conditions for Grutolla's release, he was indicted and the dispute was removed to the jurisdiction of the supreme court. There he was arraigned before Judge George Postel, who set his bail at $25,000.

Not a whisper of protest was heard from the police, even though Grutolla met the bail and, as the police theory went, was free to do "the same thing again." Judges Kleiman and Postel are both white. The reactions the press, the police, and the public established in burning italics that so far as society was concerned, a black judge should understand his enslaved place.

My assignment to night court during the Christmas and New Year holidays was in itself an interesting piece of racial punishment. One of the veteran clerks in the court, seeing me appear for duty in that last week of December, exclaimed, "Jesus Christ, I've been here for over thirty years and this is the first time I have ever seen a Christian judge here for the Christmas holidays." He had automatically assumed that I was a Christian because, except for those emotional radicals who accepted Islam and changed their names, American blacks seem to pay allegiance to the same Christianity as the slaveowners. In fact, I subscribe to no Christian or other sect. The court administrators simply assumed that I did.

The practice had always been, however, that the Jewish judges did duty on Jewish holidays. The administrators further assumed that I must be made to pay a price and learn a lesson for my bail policies, which caused them so much distress by focusing attention on their system.

Michael Dontzin, now a state supreme court judge but then counsel to Mayor John Lindsay, stopped me in the street one day. In what he must have regarded as the friendliest of ways, he said to me, "What the hell is wrong with you, Bruce? When you and Howard Rothwax were appointed, you were two of Lindsay's stars." He then warned that I was jeopardizing any chance of promotion because of my bail policies. "Settle down" was his last remonstrative advice to me.

Later, after the inauguration of the infamous Rockefeller laws regarding narcotics, the then governor was making wholesale appointments of acting Supreme Court justices to preside over the increasing number of narcotics prosecutions. At that time, Dontzin had felt it necessary to explain why I would have been one of the appointees, had I been obedient to his earlier warnings to "settle down."

I accepted the holiday assignment without protest. It was my job. Nevertheless, I was well aware of what the court administrators were doing. Any time a judge offends the administrators by public criticism, they simply give the offending judge what is regarded as a harsh assignment or one thought to be disagreeable. For me, it was the kind of abuse without due process that white employers have long been able to inflict on powerless blacks with impunity.

Earlier, I had been assigned to a court in Brooklyn, although almost without exception Manhattan judges are kept in that borough. Weary one day of hearing the district attorney's office answer the call of the day's calendar by saying that the People were ready for trial, although both he and I knew that a particular case would not be reached that day, I made an announcement from the bench. I stated in plain English that most of the defendants were either black or Puerto Rican and poor, that some of them had jobs; that the district attorney should learn who was employed and stop taking the defendants away from their work when they knew that the cases of those persons could not possibly be reached for trial; and that by missing a number of days of work the defendants would inevitably be discharged and be cast on the public dole, becoming a burden on the taxpayer's purse.

I concluded by saying that cases answered ready but not actually prepared then to proceed to trial, would be dismissed. This was immediately translated into, "So long as I am on the bench, no blacks or Puerto Ricans will ever serve time."

Shortly thereafter, I was struck by the fact that while police officers invariably described the race of each defendant as the prosecution's testimony was given. It seldom varied. "I observed the male, white Puerto Rican perpetrator," it would go. It seemed that all one needed to avoid the jeopardy of being black was to have a Spanish surname, for, all too often, the "male white Puerto Rican perpetrator" was quite as black as any of those known as black. I asked several officers if they had been instructed to make such descriptions in their Police Academy training and each said yes. I then proceeded to dismiss a series of cases for mistaken identification since the Hispanics were as dark as I am. Naturally, this conduct was dutifully reported to the district attorney, who called David Ross, then the new Administrative Judge for the city's courts. I was summarily transferred to Manhattan.

Brooklyn's supervisory judge (there is one for each county) said that as long as he, Ludwig C. Glowa, was on the bench, I would never again sit in Brooklyn. Alas, poor Glowa was not to sit there much longer. He felt the sting of the law when he was indicted for alleged bribe-taking, an indictment that was subsequently dismissed but only after it had done its pernicious mischief.

When I protested my summary removal and demanded an investigation, Ross said, with a pious and impeccable imitation of Ananias, that he had already conducted an investigation and that everything was in order.

I asked how there could have been an investigation if no one had asked me any questions. This remark was taken as impertinent and brushed aside.

I then said that the only reason for my transfer was a telephoned request from the district attorney in Brooklyn, which suggested that the district attorney, not the administrators, ran the court system.

Ross exploded, denying that he knew Eugene Gold, the district attorney, although referring to him as a "piss ant" in the same breath.

Ross concluded his interview with me (which I had been compelled to demand) by using the most vulgar and profane language imaginable. He seemed incurably coarse in his cigar-smoking resemblance to a Class "B" actor imitating a benevolent tough guy. Despite his South Bronx origins, he appeared to have no understanding or feel for sociology, relishing only his role as a "boss." After assuring me that because I was a Manhattan judge, I belonged in Manhattan, he immediately had me transferred to duty in the Bronx.

Ross is an interesting character. He is a short and affable man to whom political preference is gospel and power a treasure. By his own admission, he escaped the harsh reality of his youthful residence in the South Bronx, although he retained its tough mannerisms of speech. During my audience with him, he was surrounded by an admiring claque of white confederates who approvingly smiled and made occasional laudatory interjections. Each looked tougher than the other, as though ready to take on roles as underworld power brokers. Their appearance was wholly destructive of the profession's claim to being one that is learned and dignified.

I had been astonished to learn that most of them were lawyers. My youthful experiences with Judge James S. Watson had fixed in my mind the image of a judge as a model of dignified propriety, careful speech, scholarship, and wisdom. After all, the law was the second oldest profession and, one hoped, clearly distinguishable from the first.

In a single outburst, David Ross destroyed the illusion of learning and shattered every concept of dignity with a demonstration of crude and wide-ranging irrelevancies. It was difficult for me to remind myself that I was in the presence of a powerful jurist. His language was riddled with a toughness of expression and colorful adjectives not generally associated with the judicial image. It was easy to feel that he was talking down to me, seeking a touchstone that would activate in me something resembling his own bluff affability. My sense of shame was late in arriving, and I sank to the same poverty-stricken level as Ross.

As I retreated from his presence, I told him that he and the system had treated me as a nigger, but he was mistaken if he believed that I was anyone's nigger. As I left, I sought to slam the door, only to be frustrated by its automatic governor, which would not permit that gesture.

After that confrontation, Ross did not speak to me again for five years. In various ways, however, he undermined administrative objectivity and subjected me to an administrative punishment without charges or a hearing. For about eighteen months I was restricted to a so-called youth part, where my sole duty was to stamp approval on the papers of young offenders who had completed counseling and qualified to have their charges dismissed in the interest of justice. I was not allowed to try cases, conduct hearings or decide motions. My "courtroom" was a tiny back room with peeling paint, infested with roaches and mice.

The Patrolmen's Benevolent Association claimed credit for my internal banishment but never relented in its efforts to have me removed from the bench. The police seemed to resent the advances of the civil rights movement and the desire for power which blacks had begun to express.

It was easy to imagine that the police were the agents of those who opposed any equality for blacks. Officers routinely stopped large and expensive cars driven by blacks, simply to harass and annoy the drivers. If a black dared drive with a white woman companion, he was especially likely to be stopped by white officers. They seemed to wish to teach blacks that they had a "place" and to remember who the boss was.

In my private practice as a lawyer, I represented many black musicians. Many of them owned large and expensive cars. Some had white wives. Often I was asked to drive a wife home from where her husband was performing. Many times, I was stopped for no real reason and questioned extensively, as officers stared at my companion.

As 1974 came to an end, I was suddenly summoned to substitute for a Jewish judge who had to leave court early to observe a holiday. As though scheduled by a disgruntled karma, a black defendant was brought before me. He was charged with an entire catalog of traffic misdemeanors and offenses. The assistant district attorney moved to dismiss some charges and allowed the defendant to plead guilty to a minor offense such as driving without a license, and this was done.

I imposed the mandatory fine and the defendant departed after being given time within which to pay. The arresting officer, obviously unhappy about the reduced charges and the relatively mild penalty, followed the defendant out of the courtroom.

I noticed some activity just outside the entrance to the courtroom but did not know what it was. Suddenly, the black defendant came rushing back in. His hair was disheveled, his face was angry, and he had the appearance of one who was at a loss without his spectacles.

He asked to be heard and said that the arresting officer had followed him and demanded the right to search him. The defendant said he would not submit. The officer had drawn his weapon, clicked off the safety, and pointed it at the defendant's head. The search was then conducted. No weapon or other contraband was discovered. The defendant said that the officer had been distressed and had remarked, "You're not going to get away that lightly," before taking his gun from its holster.

After the officer conferred with the district attorney the latter said that the officer had wished to search the defendant to protect the court personnel because he knew the defendant had been charged a number of times with possession of a dangerous weapon. He concluded that the officer had taken proper police action.

In some heat, I asked the officer how he was protecting the court when, knowing the defendant's record, he waited to make the search after the defendant had left the courtroom. There was no answer. It became clear to me that personal petulance and irrationality had caused the officer to act in a rash and reckless manner. I stated that I had been sickened by the killing of ten-year-old Clifford Grover, a black child, by a white police officer, not to mention the deaths of other blacks at the hands of trigger-happy officers. I added that something drastic should be done about killer cops and those who seemed on the verge of becoming such, especially those making their targets black flesh and life.

I suggested that this officer should be deprived of his weapon. His consequent flush appeared to signal the onset of an apoplectic seizure, and I refused to listen to anything else. His immediate complaint, through the PBA, was made to the Judiciary

Relations Committee of the Appellate Division. It demanded that I be removed from the bench, and I began another series of the appearances I was to make before that grim-faced committee, a well-dressed assemblage of star-chamber functionaries who never permitted an accused judge to confront his accuser.

To come before such a body is to believe that humanity's sense of humanity has all but fled. Each judge and lawyer on the committee sat with piles of papers and transcripts before him. An official court reporter sat near the head of the table, ready to record each syllable. It was obvious that they were all impressed with the power of the PBA and its complaint that I had offended one of its members. But no matter what charge was against me, the committee always focused on the subject of bail, as though the exercise of my judicial discretion in releasing defendants before their trial was an unwritten crime in itself.

In my anger at such a gross trespass on my time and sense of dignity, I bridled at appearing before people who seemed not to know anything about the reality of judging the underworld in that arena known as the Criminal Court.

The committee seemed never to shrink from its addiction to the belief that a judge should be presumed guilty from the outset. I was just another black defendant. On the occasions when I appeared before the committee, there were always at least two black members; one, Herbert B. Evans, had been, as mentioned previously, one of my law partners.

The hearing strayed from the PBA complaint and wandered off into an inquisition into words spoken by me in public speeches and law school lectures. I had always harped on the apartheid of South Africa as compared with the constitutional apartheid I perceived in the American way of life. In a lecture at the New York Law School on the disparity in sentencing and the harshness of sentences imposed on blacks and Hispanics, as opposed to those imposed on whites, I commented on the change in the population of the state's prisons in recent years from white to black and Spanish. I said that the prisons of New York had become "black and Hispanic zoos, with mostly white keepers."

The committee suggested that that was not a proper comment for a sitting judge to make to a law school audience. I had always imagined that students of law should be exposed to the realities of the profession. I was admonished to mind my tongue in the future. It was made plain to me that I was not to exercise freedom of speech and that the First Amendment's guarantees stopped at the courthouse door—even though I had never made such remarks in a courtroom.

My lecture was thought worthy by Congressmen Herman Badillo and Charles Rangel, however, and they caused its entire text to be published in an issue of the *Congressional Record*. The *New York Law Journal* also published the remarks under the headline, "An Angry Judge Speaks Out."

This incident occurred at about the same time that Judge William F. Suglia was brought before the same Committee on Judicial Relations. Suglia is white. He had invited a black woman to his chambers and there, with overtures she found offensive, they discussed charges against her nephew. She reported this incident to the office of the Administrative Judge.

In a subsequently arranged rendezvous with the judge, the woman taped some of his proposals. For this offense, Suglia was censured; that is, a negative mention was entered into his record as a judge. It made me wonder what would happen to me if I invited a white woman to my chambers and made offensive overtures to her.

***

Dennis Brogan, the English sociologist, once described America as an "air-conditioned nightmare." I wondered why I could not make such an understated summary of America, since

I, at least, had had the experience that could have compelled this diagnosis of the country's ethos. Perhaps I was too busy with the experience of life in living color.

I had some time before perceived American reaction to color to be synonymous with a conspiracy to de-develop the black persona and keep blacks so busy defending their right to exist that all of their energies would be diverted and they would thus retrogress, becoming officially, the American untouchables, its aboriginals, caught in a static posture of nonevolvement.

We were not even supposed to reach the status of that exceptional African whom the French colonial masters contemptuously referred to as the *"evolue."*

5

Judged by the Judges

I have found it extremely difficult to converse with whites who bitterly oppose what they call quotas, reverse discrimination, and preferential treatment. They can be expected to begin each statement by announcing that they are not opposed to antidiscrimination laws to prevent future deprivations based on racial prejudice. But they seem unable to understand that the past remains with us, prejudice and bias must still be fought, and that the law needs to lead the way in preventing those who might discriminate from doing so.

Many whites do not believe legislative atonement in the present is necessary to rule out the racist abominations that have haunted America like a vindictive ghost. The only problem with this guilt rationale is that very little may be said to be "past." The past is the present, and so far as any analyst of emotional defects can detect, it will remain so as long as white eyes can perceive a darker skin color and find in that difference some comfort of superiority.

The historical comfort of the illusion inspires the racial animus and makes it seem both necessary and proper. It is as though the opening words of T. S. Eliot's *Burnt Norton* have been made the religion of race in America, for "Time present and time past / Are both perhaps present in time future. / And time future contained in the past." As Daniel Patrick Moynihan put it before he succumbed to the cant of his political ambitions, whites have castrated blacks for so long that they need not do it anymore because the blacks now do it themselves.

Now and then, blacks yield to an instinctive impulse to fight back. Sometimes they pick the wrong target. That urge was brought home forcefully to me during an incident early in my career on the bench.

I had been told that I should use every free moment unobtrusively to enter the courtrooms of older judges and learn by observing how to conduct the affairs of criminal justice. This I did with some astonishing results.

One day in the Bronx, I saw eight Hispanics brought from the detention pens to be charged and arraigned. With them was one lone black, and it was he upon whom the courtroom attention was fixed, because he repeated in a shrill and incredulous voice, "I don't shoot no craps with no spics!"

He was heedless of the decorum and dignified quiet that is supposed to attend proceedings in a court of law. He was shaking his head from side to side, repeating the same phrase. He continued his plaint while all the defendants stood before the bench.

The presiding judge said to the man's public-defender lawyer, "Counsel, will you please direct your client not to talk?" His lawyer cautioned him to say nothing. The other defendants looked at him as though they regarded him as insane. They said nothing, and a Spanish interpreter apparently did not explain the unhappy repetitions. Cautioned again to remain silent, the black became angrier, and with even greater emphasis he insisted, "But I don't shoot craps with no spics!"

The judge, showing his first sign of impatience, said to the man's lawyer, "Counselor, please tell your client what my name is." Before he could do so, the black defendant said, "All I was doing was walking along the block, trying to pass these spics shooting craps on the sidewalk, when all these cops jumped out of cars and rounded up all of us, but I *know* I don't shoot no craps with spics."

His lawyer then said to the defendant, "That's Judge Gomez." The defendant immediately exclaimed, "Oh shit, *another* spic!"

Judge Gomez, with a half-smile and shaking his head as though bewildered, said, "Dismissed, dismissed, get him out of here." The defendant left, still muttering his personal code about his choice of dicing companions, as though it was an inflexible ethic.

In a sense, the dismissal was an example of a beneficial discrimination, a competition of discriminations, or perhaps a discriminatory benefit for the black defendant. It left me with the melancholy impression that I had just witnessed, in microcosm, the war between New York City's two principal ethnic minorities.

There is another phase to that informal and official undeclared war, which has spread into the state prisons and municipal jails as well. The conflict between the blacks and Puerto Ricans has been fed and induced for many years by the Police Department. The lightest-skinned black arrested, if he has an English name, is always described as either "Black" or "Negro." From my first trial on, I was constantly amazed to notice that on the forms prepared by the arresting officers, Hispanics were invariably described as "White," no matter what their obvious pigmentation might be.

I wearied of that senseless game early in my career. I perceived, in its blindness to reality, a police conspiracy, inadvertent or otherwise, to keep the blacks and Puerto Ricans divided by reinforcing distance and hostility between them.

The result was the destruction of any possible unity between the two principal minorities and poor of the city. It seemed sad that neither group appeared to recognize that both were caught in the same ethnic trap and that discrimination against them differed, if at all, only in nuance. Unfortunately, it appeared that the Hispanics, having been described as white, had come to believe that forlorn fiction.

Whether a conspiracy or not, the practice of designating Hispanics as white was succeeding as an element of divisiveness. It was the old colonial device of divide and rule by keeping New York's blacks and Hispanics at odds. The police, acting as tools of a class their employment would never permit them to join, were perpetuating a class system within a class system. The equality of poverty was being divided into the scorned and the more scorned, even among themselves.

It reminds me of the American Colonization Society, which was organized in 1817 to establish a colony in Africa to which formerly imported Negroes in America could be exported. The society represented white fear of the black population, expressed by Thomas Jefferson, that one day the Negroes would rise up to redress the grievances of slavery.

In the twentieth century, the notion of exporting the dark menace has been replaced by internal methods of division and containment. The political triumphs of blacks in major cities such as Atlanta and New Orleans symbolize the power of black unity. If the blacks and Hispanics were ever to compromise their differences and vote for a common purpose, they easily could win the mayor's office and many others. The police remain the agents of ethnic division in New York City even though, ironically, most of them seem to be nonresidents.

The underlying act of dividing the black and Puerto Rican communities continues in a different form, for now it appears that blacks with Spanish surnames are referred to as "Hispanics" and only occasionally as "whites."

Judged by the Judges

There must be relatively few charges of racism brought against white judges at official disciplinary proceedings. I would assume that white judges would consider a charge of racism a minor accusation. A black judge so charged might find his situation more precarious.

One night, as I sat in the newly established Bronx Criminal Court, a young district attorney named Martin Schwartz was on duty. He seemed tense, and the quick, darting movement of both his eyes and gestures as well as his manner of speech gave him a furtive appearance.

During a break in the proceedings, he came to my robing room to talk. He told me that he had worked in Washington as a Treasury agent, investigating and discovering evidence for criminal prosecutions by the federal government. He was not happy in that role because he never did the prosecuting, and what he really wished to do was try cases. So he had resigned and joined the staff of the Bronx district attorney, then Burton Roberts.

In a moment of revelation, Schwartz touched on the District of Columbia's preventive detention ordinance for holding someone charged with a crime until the time of the trial. I asked if this was not President Nixon's idea of controlling the mostly black population of Washington by undermining the presumption of innocence.

He ignored that question but responded that every white person in America harbored some bias and prejudice against blacks and that, on the basis of what he had seen, he understood and felt some sympathy for the John Birch Society. I was astonished at this admission, but both of us were called back to duty before the subject could be further explored.

Shortly after court resumed, a black man was arraigned before me. As I recall, he was charged with attempted murder and possession of a dangerous weapon. Separated from his wife and small child, he had gone to their former home to deliver alimony or child support.

Because he was employed as a security guard, he carried a weapon. He surprised his wife, his lawyer said, *in flagrante delicto* with another man, while his little daughter was in the same room. His fury ignited, he attempted to shoot at his wife's lover, who fled, half clad. The shot had missed. The man's lawyer, well known to me, vouched for his client's integrity, and both promised that, if released, the defendant would return to court on the date set.

I said that he would be released on his given word.

Schwartz became excited and angry, demanding bail of $25,000 as a condition of the defendant's pretrial release. I said the matter was concluded and that the next case should be presented. Schwartz, however, continued to press for the requested bail.

The exchange became heated. I reminded Schwartz that he had confessed to me his own sense of bias and said I feared his demonstration to be proof of his own prejudice. He and a companion, Howard Finger, immediately complained to both the press and the Committee on Judiciary Relations.

Schwartz summoned Burton Roberts himself. Roberts appeared and asked to speak to me in chambers. Roberts is a strange and flamboyant personality, best described as an unusual character. Neither he nor his peculiar characteristics were unknown to me. He had been a roommate of my tennis partner at Cornell Law School and, from time to time, we met socially.

I remembered his crestfallen appearance when he applied for employment at the firm of Proskauer, Rose, Goetz & Mendelsohn where I was then working. The firm insisted that each associate bring with him or her the intellectual distinction of having been a law review editor. Roberts did not meet that standard. Rejected in his ambition, he wrote a lengthy and rambling letter, the main theme of which was that when he was where the bombs were falling during World War II, no one had required him to be a law review editor.

138

Roberts had refined his personal vision of the imitation of life to reflect the image of what he believed a film version of a district attorney should be. His facial expressions varied from a skeptical squint to a cunning half-smile as though he had just received a printout of an adversary's mind.

Affecting his best Hollywood style, he insisted upon privacy with me. "Listen, Bruce," he said "even if you're correct in dealing with Schwartz, and I doubt it, I would still have to protect my man." He then added a comment about my bail practices, saying, "That crap may be all right in Manhattan, but not up here."

This was his way of confirming that the Bronx was his personal fiefdom and that I was at best a licensed trespasser. He ignored my lecture to him about my determination not to tolerate any intrusion of racist bias in any court where I sat.

Earlier in my career, when I had been general counsel to the Human Resources Administration of the City of New York, I had to appear at ceremonies celebrating the opening of community law offices. On one such occasion in the Bronx, Roberts and I were chatting backstage before being called upon to speak. Roberts was in rare and eloquent form as he damned the United States Supreme Court for its decisions under Chief Justice Warren, who, he said, adeptly using the current cliché, had handcuffed the police and prosecutors.

In his actual address, Roberts launched into extravagant praise of the very court opinions he had just cursed. The subject of a 1969 *New York* magazine article, he had been featured in a full-face photograph on the magazine's cover, with a legend that portrayed him as the city's "toughest D.A." Inside, it was as though a coarse comedian had granted an interview by acting out some of his more censorable material.

At one point, Roberts discussed blacks. He became a darky in white-face, and his voice was transformed into minstrel intonations as he assured the author of the article that there was no

139

trouble from the "schvartzes" 'cause they knows they's gonna end up in the pokey." All of this was acted out with the flashing eyes and showing of teeth that Roberts attributed to blacks.

The following week, a letter from a Mr. Fishman appeared in the magazine, asking how anyone could have respect for the law when the highest law officer of the Bronx used the Yiddish term for "niggers" in referring to blacks. As though not to slight the Hispanics by omitting any mention of their status, he later commented to the press about a political dispute involving Puerto Ricans by suggesting that they were savages and the Bronx itself a jungle.

Roberts appears to be restless as a State Supreme Court justice. All too often, it seems that he has relinquished the title of district attorney but not the role. Judges presiding at jury trials are supposed to be aloof from bias and take no sides. Indeed, a standard part of a judge's instructions to a jury is the admonition that the judge himself has no opinion about the case being tried because that is the territorial imperative of the jury. Nevertheless, Roberts has been reversed several times in murder cases for intruding his views into a trial.

In an October 1980 reversal of a jury verdict of guilty in a murder trial, the Appellate Division in Manhattan noted that Mr. Justice Roberts had asked questions of witnesses in such a way that his skepticism was revealed. This "persuasive error," the court wrote, "deprived the defendant of a fair trial." A new and expensive trial was ordered. In 1979, the manslaughter convictions of two defendants were reversed because Justice Roberts had asked thirteen hundred questions, more than one-third of all the questions posed during the trial.

In a 1978 bribe-receiving trial, a federal court annulled the conviction of the defendant because he felt that the conduct of the trial judge (Roberts) would lead to his conviction in any event. And in another 1978 case, in which manslaughter was

140

charged, an appeals court reversed a conviction because, as it said, Roberts had "unduly injected himself" into the trial.

Such injections are like adrenalin to Roberts. He will never be a truly happy public servant until he is once again a district attorney, possessed of a perfect right to demonstrate with flamboyance and flair what side he is on. The remarks he made to me concerning the Schwartz incident were no surprise. It would have been surprising had he been quietly analytical and understanding.

For my scolding of Schwartz, I was summoned before a Judiciary Relations Committee, which had heard testimony in my absence to which I was never allowed access. Both Martin Schwartz and Howard Finger had given their versions of what had occurred.

The committee members posed oblique questions, obviously in an effort to catch me up in some harmful inconsistency. The atmosphere was hostile. Everyone but I had a transcript of the official court minutes of my exchanges with Schwartz. Suddenly, though, it occurred to my learned inquisitors that it was perhaps awkward to press upon me questions related to an event that had occurred months earlier while they looked at an official record of the event and I had none. To the embarrassment of some of the committee members, it was moved that they go into executive session while I was allowed to read the transcript. It took only a few minutes after my testimony for the committee to dictate its findings and censure me for my remarks "on the record" to Schwartz. The inference could be drawn that for similar but off-the-record remarks, there would have been prosecution.

Earlier I had attempted to get the very transcript that had been withheld from me, only to be told by the official court reporter that he had instructions not to prepare one for me. The infamous "star chamber" had served as a useful precedent for the judges to utter their opinion of me.

Another interesting aspect of the committee's work is the presence among its members of Herbert B. Evans, who later became the state's chief Administrative Judge. His functions there did not seem entirely clear, except as the author of frequent memoranda transmitting the views of the chief judge of the Court of Appeals who had selected him.

Evans, intellectually gifted and an ultraconservative with a devotion to murky detail, had been one of my former law partners. He and I had never been close friends and had, indeed, been at odds for most of the time we practiced law in the same firm. In view of our past friction, I was mildly astonished that he insisted on sitting in judgment of me rather than withdrawing.

It seemed natural that he would one day become, in effect, the state's controlling analyst of judicial ethics because he ignored the caution urged upon all judges to avoid even the appearance of impropriety. Not only did Evans persist in his committee membership, but he joined in the unanimous censure of me for my remarks to Schwartz.

One other black judge had served on the committee, William Loguen, but he had so fully passed over into the white ranks that few blacks were aware that he was nominally one of them. In skin color he was so fair as to deceive the American eye's usual eagerness to detect the single drop of black blood that marked one as a Negro.

Loguen had been a longtime prosecutor before elevation to the bench, and he and I had only a nodding acquaintance. If the rumor is accurate that this man is related to the Rev. J. W. Loguen, an escaped slave, he is proof of the theory that genes of resistance can be diluted through the years by the token comforts of the system.

Rev. Loguen not only escaped to Syracuse but in March of 1860 wrote a testy letter to his former owner, chastising her for demanding money from him and for having sold his brother and sister. It must be one of the few examples in history of angry correspondence between former slave and master.

By 1972, however, the militance that had inspired Reverend Loguen's 1850s escape to Syracuse and later to Canada obviously no longer existed in the Loguen bloodline. William Loguen had become as remote from his forebears as most white judges are from each other. It is proof, I suppose, of the observation that it is grand to be well descended, but that the glory belongs to the ancestors.

Following the complaint against me by the PBA and the censure of the Judiciary Relations Committee, my life on the bench changed drastically, and I was beset by doubts whether I should continue in a career I had never hoped or prepared for. The threats to my life continued apace, as did the deluge of racist condemnation in signed and unsigned letters and cards.

I continued to endure the status of a well-paid but not very trusted clerk. I sat in review of reports made by counselors, which recommended either dismissal or criminal charges or a further period of counseling. I stamped papers and spoke fatherly clichés to young offenders.

Had it not been for the friendship of Eugene Hanley, the Youth Part clerk, I would have done practically no judicial work for almost eighteen months. He recognized what the administration of David Ross was doing, as it seemed to yield to the strident demands of the police that I be controlled and isolated from all work involving the setting of bail.

Hanley, feigning an innocent eagerness to help those judges whose parts were overburdened with long calendars, surreptitiously brought cases to me for hearings and motions. I would conduct such proceedings in a sub rosa atmosphere, as though doing the business of a secret court. For his outspoken expressions of sympathy for my plight and his independence of mind, Hanley was transferred to different duty in a part of the city as distant from his home as municipal boundaries would allow. He has since retired to the kindlier bleakness of a rural Rhode Island address.

My fellow judges accepted my banishment as normal, and if they discussed it at all, they did so outside the hearing of my friendly spies. Their mute tolerance of my treatment was a tribute to the blindness of their focus on personal ambition. Those who spoke to me at all advised against harsh criticism of the system, pointing to the dictatorial power of the court administrators.

When Leo Milonas became the Supervisory Judge of the Manhattan Criminal Court, he looked in on my dirty little backwater of a Youth Part one day and said, "Jesus, Bruce, you've been here so long. Don't you want a change of assignment?"

I had known Milonas when we were both practicing law, and I said, "I dare you to give me some judicial duties."

My next assignment was to a Jury Part. The assignment was listed for a month. It lasted just two weeks. Milonas was overruled, and I was sent back to the Youth Part. From there I was summoned to an arraignment part because of the absence during a religious holiday of the judge then presiding. And it was there that I admonished the officer who had needlessly drawn his weapon and held it close to the head of a black defendant.

Ten years after my appearance before the Committee on Judiciary Relations, I received a remarkable letter from the man who had prosecuted me so enthusiastically. He wrote that he owed me "an apology long overdue," for his role as the committee's counsel "in the investigation conducted against you." He said that he had seen two movies (*The Year of Living Dangerously* and *Bananas*) that made him examine certain premises he held about "Law and order, racism and the terrible forces sometimes unjustly unleashed" by the government and "certain ugly segments of the press against individuals who rock the boat to upset the establishment." He recalled that there "was an hysterical mob screaming for my blood" for being reminded how "racism still lives like a cancer in society."

He then spoke of society treating "poor blacks accused of crimes as 'niggers' " and "caged animals." He then concluded by writing that instead of an investigation of the "horrible conditions" I inveighed against, "the focus was on the 'injudicial language' " used by me. The investigation and prosecution of charges against me were, he said, a "miserable episode," and he asked for forgiveness for his role in it.

6

Quotas and Quarrels

Some expression of the attitudes of my colleagues toward me was made public at a Hunter College seminar for trial judges, a program administered by a former Civil Court judge, Edward Goodell. He asked that I deliver a lecture touching on aspects of racism as they affected criminal justice.

I prepared my notes, cited some courthouse graffiti, and added some personal views concerning black judges and their slim numbers. I had twenty minutes to make my points before being exposed to questions from an audience of judges who, if friendly, successfully suppressed any evidence of that emotion.

There was tentative laughter when I quoted a piece of wall writing that had been just outside the Youth Part for more than a year. It referred to a television commercial for tuna fish, in which a garrulous character named Charlie Tuna was never chosen by a company that insisted (in its commercials at least) on only the finest quality. The commercial showed Charlie being caught and cast back into the sea. The legend on the wall read:

"Charlie Tuna must be a nigger fish, he's so socially unacceptable."

I mention this anecdote for a reason. In the halls outside the courtroom, youthful defendants who had been released on bail or their own recognizance while being counseled often milled about exchanging stories and their personal views of judges and justice. They smoked, discussed the possibilities of their impending fate, and often debated with their lawyers the competing merits of what options they might have. It is in the halls that practical and piercing insights are expressed concerning justice.

Lenny Bruce summed it all up in his bitter observation, "In the halls of justice, justice is in the halls." That, too, has become a part of the wall literature of the Criminal Court.

Although it contains no mention of race, the blacks and Puerto Ricans who can read have allowed their street wisdom to adopt the aphorism. They see it applicable to their circumstance. They believe as soon as they enter the courtroom, the judge will show nothing but wrath. They express the view there is no such thing as an honest judge. They seem to wish to be brought before one of their peers, a judge who is an urban peasant, handing out benevolent dismissals.

The Charlie Tuna graffiti remained undisturbed for several years. It could be easily read. It was in what Arthur Koestler has described as the neat and legible script of the illiterate.

In my speeches and lectures, I have never neglected an opportunity to point out that although 85 to 90 percent of the Criminal Court defendants are blacks and dark Hispanics, there was not a single black or Hispanic Supervisory Judge in any of the five boroughs of the city for many years.

Because I hammered at this theme, suggesting that there was distrust of black and Hispanic judges, it was felt in the office of David Ross, the Administrative Judge for the entire city, that I was somehow betraying private club secrets. One of his closest administrative assistants, the late Archie Gorfinkel, was a burly, hulking figure of a man. He was a natural ally of his boss. His faults of personality were matched by his loud manner of speech and blunt expression. His appearance made him a perfect candidate for typecasting.

One day, as I ate lunch in a restaurant near the courts, my table was near one at which he sat. Upon seeing me, he leaped suddenly to his feet. With a menacing flourish, which caused other diners to fall silent, he point an accusing finger at me, while yelling at the top of his voice, "You tell lies in your speeches; you're nothing but a liar and you know it!"

He had seized on the fact that Jawn Sandifer, a black, was Ross's deputy in charge of the city's Criminal Courts and the Criminal Divisions of the Supreme Court. He pointed to Sandifer as support for his public accusation that I had lied when I said that there was neither a black nor a Hispanic supervisory judge in any of the five boroughs.

There could have been no more dramatic a demonstration of how Gorfinkel had risen to the height of inaccuracy. He well knew that at the time I had spoken, there was not a single black or Hispanic supervisory judge in each of the five criminal courts of the five boroughs. But facts were obviously irrelevant to him.

Sandifer was not a "supervisory" judge, but a deputy assistant administrative judge for the city and all of its boroughs. Such a scene was a demonstration of fealty to his then superior, more than to accuracy. Having been a supervisory judge in the Bronx, Gorfinkel became an acting Supreme Court justice.

After my remarks before the judges at the Hunter College clinical seminar, the first questions fired at me was from M. Marvin Berger. He and I had received appointments to the bench at the same time. He had at one time been general counsel to the *New York Post* before its decline into tabloid sensationalism. I assumed him to be a man of great wisdom. Instead of the promised question, however, he elected to make a speech.

Aiming his finger unerringly at me, he accused me of "basic dishonesty" in saying that of the one hundred judges of the Criminal Court, none of the supervisory judges was black and only some ten judges were black. To my amazement, he then said, "There are only 98 on the Criminal Court. You know there are not 100."

I have long been vexed by the large numbers of black and Puerto Rican defendants in the Criminal Court, and when pressed by questioners as to why, I have sought to wrestle with elusive answers. It seems there are many more advisory services available to whites who still reside in the city or who are arrested there. Advice is available through religious organizations or other social service groups. Seldom does a white Catholic youth, for example, appear before the arraignment bar without a representative either of his church or of some other group to vouch for his stability and trustworthiness in returning to court when needed.

Such representatives give the court a sense of trust in looking after the defendant and offering help while his case is pending.

Invariably, such support results in the defendant's pre-trial release. Often, it also results in a reduction of the charges and, sometimes, their eventual dismissal. Support services also exist for the few Jewish defendants who are caught up in the system of criminal justice.

In New York, most of the white Protestants have fled elsewhere for a variety of reasons, including a public school system that is overwhelmingly black and Puerto Rican and thus subject to cruel and heedless treatment by those who run it. The white Protestants have also avoided the changing neighborhoods which, through what the sociologists have called succession and invasion, have become darker and darker as the so-called inner city has spread like an ethnic Rorschach.

The Protestants in New York City today are, in the main, black. And, despite the ever-increasing number of charismatic, pentecostal, and emotional sects among the Hispanics who are Protestant, the Protestant Federation has abdicated any activist role in fending for them. The federation has become the private club of a handful of brooding do-gooders. It justifies its existence as a social agency by having meetings and box lunches calculated not to offend urban peasants.

There are always a few token blacks on the board, but because this membership serves only to certify its middle-class visions, whatever is social about the federation seems restricted to its internecine gatherings. I served on the board briefly when it was thought mistakenly that I was a Protestant.

The failure of the Protestant church to meet its obligations to its black members is a scandal. Protestants could be kept busy providing to black defendants the counseling and court assistance that is routinely available to Catholic and Jewish defendants. This lack in the lives of young black Protestants helps increase the deprivation of choices and options that the minority poor might otherwise have. My expression of some of these views at the Hunter College seminar met with bitter disagreement among my fellow speakers and questioners.

Some of these critics voiced opinions later to be developed by Charles H. Silberman. In a 1978 book, *Criminal Violence: Criminal Justice*, he seems to attribute the large number of black criminal defendants to an innate savagery and an instinctive racial compulsion. He then writes that he is astonished by black violence because the poor black creatures captured in Africa and sold into slavery were gentle; violence, he says, was not a part of their baggage, as though blacks made happy landfalls in America as African tourists, instead of as kidnapped contraband.

Silberman offers no mention of slavery's dreadful insult to American piety and the Constitution. Neither does he engage the terrible penalty even now being imposed on the generations coming after slavery and its abolition. One finds in his acid pages no criticism of the United States Constitution, which American

151

history describes as the most perfect instrument for governance ever drawn by the hand of man.

His pages are bereft of sensitive consideration either of cause or consequence of the black circumstance in the centuries of white Christian deprivation and degradation represented by slavery, or in the post-emancipation years of benighted and tethered human intercourse, so blemished by the sight of skin color and so much a flawed replica of the apartheid holding sway in South Africa.

My constant jeopardy arising from accusations against me began to be a matter of acute concern to my family and to myself as well. I began to feel completely isolated, a pariah, avoided by my colleagues as though I had become a leper. It was then that I began to think of a new career and to deplore the day I had given up my practice to join the Lindsay Administration.

The realization of powerlessness in the face of threat can be a forceful catalyst for self-pity and fruitless anger. It occurred to me that, at my time of life, I needed no such nonsense as the unending stream of racist letters and anonymous promises of maiming and death.

My fellow members of the bench stood mute, failing to appreciate that if the administration could treat me in a special way, they, too, could become victims. It was a lonely battle to oppose those in whose hands the fate of one's career rested. This was especially true in my case because I belonged to no political party and had no friends in places of power.

In retrospect, I understand the acidity of a passage from *The Gift of Chaos,* by Dr. Anna Arnold Hedgeman. She mentions the complete divestment of relationship and personality felt by black Africans brought to this country in slave ships and placed among strangers in a hostile land. They came without passports, without visas, without tickets of passage and without knowledge of direction or destination. It was ridiculous then to expect blacks to celebrate the bicentennial, as it would have approved the scandal of Christians owning slaves under a Constitution and its glorious mentions of freedom.

Some reservations surfaced during the extravagant adoration of the Statute of Liberty and its centennial. One hundred years ago, a large part of this country was busy undoing reconstruction and the post-Civil War constitutional amendments. During my ordeal by harassment and being ignored and avoided by my colleagues, I felt I was an actor in a foreign-language drama. I could not define my role and, in any case, there was no audience. My efforts at escape only worsened my sense of exile.

I allowed my name to be considered as a law instructor at the New York University Law School. I was told by the black students who urged my cause that some of the school expressed the belief that I was too old to undertake such a new career. It seemed alien to their mission, somehow, for those associated with a law school to abuse the law by discriminating against someone because of age. In my early fifties, I seemed to have become an outcast for reasons both of age and racial impertinence.

The PBA intensified its barrage in the effort to have me unfrocked. Kenneth McFeeley and, before him, Robert McKiernan, as PBA presidents, had used vituperation against me as a means of achieving popularity with their association and election to office. Both had pledged to work unceasingly to have me drummed off the bench. They detested my criticism of trigger-happy officers to whom blacks had become a target and who shot to kill when confronted by blacks.

I deplored the killer instinct seemingly aroused in so many white police officers by the sight of black skin. I expressed the view that New York had deteriorated into a police state where no white police officer would ever be convicted for the slaying of a black.

Newspapers and television reporters had taken up the term "Turn 'Em Loose Bruce" as a derogatory title, making capital of public fear and hysteria over crime. Editorials abounded in their harsh criticism of me, revealing a deep ignorance of the criminal justice system and the Constitution itself. The few favorable comments in the press never received the prominence of the negative reports.

It seemed that I was being told that, for this black judge at least, there was no such thing as a First Amendment right to free speech. The attempt to stop my protests was all the more interesting because my most severe remarks had not been made from the bench or even the courthouse.

I was astonished to be told that a law school forum, for example, was an improper place to discuss controversy and that such conduct would expose me to a wide range of severe penalties. I had no idea how the law could escape dispute, investigation, debate, contradiction, and a ceaseless inquiry, made with the zeal of an honest quest.

Donald Shapiro, the Dean of New York Law School, sought me out for a position on the law school's adjunct faculty. By a vote of three to two, the faculty committee turned me down. Dean Shapiro suggested there should be another try later because he had been absent on business when the vote came up. Had the vote been reversed, it would have been little better for me because it suggested that I would be transferring my vulnerability to another arena of enmity. Anyway, as I told Shapiro, I would have been at that time but a sorry token, the one quota black.

Naturally, few bigots concede that their rulings are made on the basis of racist animus. Even some white judges had long ago noticed that persons and institutions will always assign a variety of discovered reasons for rejection of blacks that have no apparent roots in racism. If a racist rejection represents an act of inhumanity, it often is nevertheless the fashionable and thus acceptable thing to do, and that makes it respectable.

I long became resigned to such explanations, although hardly immune. My own impression of what the sight of color can do to a white mind had begun with my exclusion from Princeton's skating rink in 1935 and shortly thereafter my rejection from Princeton University itself.

That was a long time ago, but changes of attitude seemed to have escaped any alteration of feelings about color in America. Michael Sovern, before he became President of Columbia University, came to my home for dinner one evening. He was then dean of the university's law school. After an exemplary meal and some exquisite red Margaux, I brought the conversation around to Alexander Hamilton and asked Sovern if Hamilton had been the first black to attend Columbia. He seemed startled by my conclusion that Hamilton had been a Negro and appeared to know nothing about the historical notion of Hamilton's shadowy West Indian background and birth on the island of Nevis.

I tried to assuage his apparent distress by assuring him that it was not the worst DNA tragedy in the world because we already knew the scandal of the first black president of the United States, Warren G. Harding.

I was giving him some dark and gossipy insights into American history as it is sometimes discussed in black neighborhoods or by historians. I recommended to him a biography of Harding in which Harding himself is quoted as asking a close friend, "Do you really think I'm part nigger?"

And then I arrived at the real point of the discussion: the controversy surrounding my career and my search for a more compatible intellectual atmosphere. I had assumed, incorrectly as it developed, that each of us was more tolerant of the other and much more mellow than in a non-alcoholic moment. I posed the ultimate question, which ruined the evening and brought about the pall of silence at a dinner table that precedes embarrassed declarations of reasons for uncomfortable guests to depart.

I said, "Mike, what are my chances for doing some adjunct teaching at the Law School?" As calmly as though he heard such questions on a daily basis from black supplicants for his favor, Sovern replied, with an even gaze at me, "But, Bruce, we already have *one.*"

Once again, I had had the old token defense, the quota limitation thrown at me. *One* was the quota. *One* was white society's favor, its generous boon, its grudging academic handout from the intellectual welfare rolls. Kellis Parker was the law school's lone black professor, and that was that. We made the usual polite goodbyes, and I have not spoken to him since. I did write to him to ask if he recalled his remark and his reply was that the quotation attributed to him sounded more like something I would say.

The sense of repugnant controversy that enveloped my professional life also spread beyond the seas. In my search for other avenues along which to express my energies, I had several interviews with a law firm in the West Indies. Just when partnership details were being discussed, eight people were killed by dissident blacks in St. Croix in the Virgin Islands.

I was told that I was too controversial and under no circumstances could I join the firm then interviewing me. I could not escape, it seemed. And in New York, the fever pitch of racist events continued.

Racism is practiced, overtly and otherwise, as instinctive ritual. It seeps into all aspects of life. It is amazing to see how many white people still cling to the pre-emancipation conviction that all Negroes look alike. It would be much less astonishing if blacks believed all whites look alike. Certainly they have a more uniform skin color than blacks.

The astonishment derives from the visual fact that since all whites are nearly the same color, it would not seem surprising if blacks must believe all whites look alike.

Clearly the color whites call black skin excites similar emotions in them. When McGeorge Bundy headed the Ford Foundation, he once summoned a number of blacks, myself included,

156

to his home on Fifth Avenue. He wanted to sample black thoughts about the restlessness of black students at Yale University. He was scheduled to go to New Haven to offer palliatives to soothe their agitation and sedate their sense of rebellion. They were deeply involved in the emotions of a Black Panther trial then just beginning, and they also wished Yale to withdraw all of its investments in South Africa.

Although I was aware of the troubled black spirit there, I had no idea that Bundy's invitation was an effort to get black ideas on how to prevent black agitation from becoming action that might embarrass Yale.

I reported precisely at the appointed Sunday afternoon hour. The doorman, an aged Irish servitor, was a starched serf who had brought to the twentieth century all of the prejudices he believed his upper-class tenants supported. He looked at me suspiciously and, with his spare and unsturdy body placed squarely in my path, demanded to know my business. In his rigid severity, he seemed to believe he was as heroic as the little Dutch boy with his finger in the dike.

My business was none of his, and I felt that he would never have asked a white visitor such a question in such a tone of hostility.

I said simply, "Tell Mr. McGeorge Bundy that Bruce Wright is on his way up."

I sought in vain to be as haughty in my attitudes as the whites whom he doubtless welcomed daily in his cherished high-rise castle.

I failed, of course, for there are few members of ancient and dynastic royalty who can be as superior as those urban peasants who are doormen for the rich. He said, "You must use the service elevator," and he called to a junior employee to show the way.

I ignored him. I was not surprised but angry. I walked straight to the passenger elevator, with its mirrors and a bench on one side. I said to the elevator man, "The Bundy apartment, please," and pretended to be preoccupied with my newspaper as I sat down.

There was a hurried discussion between agitated uniformed men. I suggested that I should be taken up immediately or that the police be called, although I had no idea what the police could do in such a situation. There was always the ponderous machinery of the State Commission on Human Rights, and I began to wonder if an elevator ride was a civil right. A white man then entered the elevator, barely looked at me, and began to read his newspaper. For *him*, the elevator man began his ascent, and I was delivered.

As I entered the Bundy apartment, my face must have reflected my anger. Bundy said, "My God, Bruce, you look like a dark cloud. What happened?" His simile did nothing to help my mood.

I described the antebellum hauteur of the doorman. He then exclaimed spontaneously, as his face clouded over and he looked at his wife, "Perhaps I should have told them before." He and his wife and an enormous dog then exited the apartment in unison, each wearing an expression of distress and anxiety. Left alone, I sought to salvage something of the afternoon by going to a window facing Central Park and musing on the birds that hovered over the nearby reservoir.

When the Bundys and their pet returned, they asked, in a make-conversation way, what I was gazing at. I asked what kind of birds were obviously having their own Sunday afternoon meeting. No one knew. I offered the opinion that they must be "local Jim Crows, perhaps." It was a gauche remark, but no less spontaneous than Bundy's, "Perhaps I should have told them." After that, the silence was almost visible as we awkwardly awaited the late arrivals.

When the others finally gathered, I had very little to say, feel-

ing that I would be something of a Quisling to aid and abet the
Bundy cause of controlling some intellectually restless black students.

I remained busy, speculating on the powerful people in
American society who are essentially stars in the strange pageant
of the country's democracy but who nevertheless allow so many
walk-ons, the extras, to be the agents of the animus which di-
minishes theories of equality.

It is in that way that a drama of gloom is authored for blacks. It
had always been so, from the time in 1789 when Thomas
Jefferson, with pious hypocrisy, had purported to hate slavery
and had even proposed freedom for the blacks at the Constitutional Convention and thereafter. He appeared to wish an egalitarian, libertarian, and revolutionary concept to apply to all.
That aim was soundly defeated.

Of course, Jefferson had set a poor example by appearing at
the convention as one of Virginia's largest slave owners. Instead
of freeing his slaves, either before or after the convention, he
returned to Monticello, brimming with Christian faith, to enjoy
his slaves, and especially his long-lasting liaison with Sally
Hemings, his black mistress. He ultimately freed his children by
Miss Hemings, but never freed her.

I mention these incidents simply to show that my experiences
should have prepared me to be astonished about nothing. And
yet both astonishment and dismay are constant trespassers on
my sense of awareness.

I assume that I suffer from a weakness of character and that
that weakness continues to dupe me into believing that people
of power (the white majority) will use influence to urge national
support for the blessings of liberty. All too often, it seems that
the fulfillment of a constitutional ideal is desired only by blacks.

It is as though the dead hand of a mortgage forecloses for
blacks those blessings so carefully spelled out in the original

Constitution for whites only. Sloan Coffin was emphatically accurate when he observed in one of his sermons that people of power have no good will and people of good will have no power.

My amazements leave me bruised. The American ethos and its enslavement to ignorance seem to compel white America to reserve its harshest treatment for citizens who are unfashionably dressed in black skin. This includes all of those beautiful and in-between colors that are not black at all but are called so only in reference to people.

All of my experiences should have provided a coarse preparation for what was to be witnessed in the court system. They were certainly numerous enough. After my first year at college, I was hired for a job as a lifeguard at the small prestigious Camp Moosehead in New Canaan, Connecticut. I dutifully reported and was welcomed by the Filipino cook, who happened to be a Bible school student.

Mrs. Jerome, who ran the camp, was obviously shocked at seeing me. "Who are you?" she asked.

When I told her that one of my professors had arranged summer work for me at the camp, she said, "There must be some mistake. We asked for a lifeguard, not another cook." She admonished me not to go into the lake under any circumstances while she sought a replacement for me. In the meantime, I was provided with a long wooden pole and instructed to sit in a rowboat and watch over the wealthy young boys as they swam.

I was given a sleeping bag and a place to sleep over a garage. The cook and I became fast friends and swam in the lake every morning and evening. I ignored Mrs. Jerome's instructions. The cook was as amused as I was about her distress.

One night, as I helped the cook while he served the Jeromes and their two sons, the telephone rang. I answered and was told that it was for Donald, one of Mrs. Jerome's sons, known as Donny.

The cook asked me to inform Donny. I looked into the dining

room and said, "Excuse me, but there's a telephone call for Donny."

Mrs. Jerome, with a startled look on her face, rose immediately, and advanced on me in a menacing manner. As we both entered the kitchen, she was livid as she shouted, "My son is Mr. Donald! Do you understand?"

I said, "Of course. If he's Mr. Donald to me, then I'm Mr. Bruce to him."

Donny could not have been more than a year or so older than I was. I was angry at this antebellum demonstration of the caste system. The next day, Mrs. Jerome summoned me to her office. She asked me if I were a communist, said she had never asked for a colored lifeguard, and told me I was discharged. She said that "Mr. Donny" would drive me to the train.

In some ways, I suppose, Camp Moosehead was like a Y.M.C.A. camp I had attended as a young boy.

In the 1930s, the Y.M.C.A. was just another institution waging pious racism, with separate facilities for blacks. It operated a camp in northern New Jersey called Camp Washington. For ten days, Negro boys were there and then, for the next ten, only whites.

As my contingent left one year, I was part of the cleanup force. The camp had to be prepared for the white campers. One of my duties was to remove the picture of Booker T. Washington from over the dining hall fireplace and put up a picture of George Washington. Booker T. had not been a slaveowner, but a slave. It was an ironic comment on theories of racial acceptance in America that a slaveowner's image was framed for white youths and that of a former slave for the blacks. That kind of suggestion must have had great influence in preserving the separate-but-equal myth.

Dealings with generations of white men failed to cure me of my naïve belief that education was the way to reform a delinquent society. And yet, the educated classes in America, and those belonging to groups that determine policy and have power, are reluctant to use their power to heal the wound that gives America so much illogical anguish.

When I came to the bench, I automatically assumed that I would be in the midst of men of great learning and dignity. I believed that they would have a sacred respect and love for the Constitution and a zealous devotion to be fair, just and objective. I neglected to take into account the emotional turbulence generated in whites when they are confronted by a black person accused of crime, especially when that accusation involves a white person as the victim.

Black individuality, emerging from the amorphous mass of unworthy darkness, seems to intensify distrust, as does my sign of black independence. The latter often results in a black being thought of as a "cheeky nigger," or worse, and there are built-in penalties for displays of what might be construed as black arrogance or self-assertion.

Despite my long basic training in the endurance of American hostility, I remain bitterly awe-stricken by the ignorance of many white judges on the subject of human relations. Perhaps my error in putting together a suitable syllogism is my underlying premises that blacks, too, are human. Many whites with whom I have had close relationships have radically stereotyped concepts about the black personality.

An impossible dream has occurred to me in which all blacks have staged a national paint-in, and every black domestic, laborer, radical, and activist has managed to sedate all whites with a secret drug and then paint them black. This, of course, is a desperately unrealizable fantasy because many black domestics seem to revere their white employers and would never think of doing anything out of character.

That black men have stood mute when their rage should have compelled them to scream, to rant, to rave, and to be insane has never ceased to amaze me. I continue to cling to the belief that those who know must speak out.

When I was still on the bench and filled with the wonder of the power that comes with a black robe and allows one to imprison others, to impose fines, and to deliver lectures on morality, I persisted in using my free time to watch the older judges do their work. Some cynics say that this is one way to compound error if such examples are followed.

Even before my career on the bench began, I would watch judges carefully. As a young lawyer, I wanted very much to know something about the judges I would be practicing before. I was not a member of any organizations, except a poor minority track and field club. I had no political influence and was not enrolled in a party. I had heard stories of how lawyers would deliberately call a judge's attention to the small symbols of freemasonry they wore in their lapels and of how that sense of fraternity often helped a cause when merit had no place.

One day, I sat with Livingston Wingate, who is now a judge, as he waited in a courtroom to seek an adjournment so that he could be elsewhere on another mission. The presiding judge was George Carney.

Because of the numerous blacks and Puerto Ricans who are defendants in the criminal courts, I was surprised to see that a white defendant stood before the bench to be sentenced, having earlier been convicted. His lawyer, also white, made an eloquent plea to Judge Carney, asking that his client be placed on probation and not sent to jail. He assured the judge that the defendant could be rehabilitated. Counsel's entire air was one of absolute certainty and knowledge, which I thought would be impossible for the judge to resist.

Judge Carney appeared to be thumbing impatiently through a pre-sentence report then before him. When the defendant's lawyer completed his argument, Carney lifted his head and vehemently snarled a concussive question: "How's he going to be rehabilitated when he's living with a colored woman?" As though the attributed criminality of such an "outrageous" and "heinous" deed required re-emphasis, Judge Carney repeated his question twice.

His first expression of the question roused in me some anger. I realized that I, too, was living with what the judge had contemptuously described as a "colored woman." There raced through my head recollections of the infamous Scottsboro case, when nine young men had been accused of raping two white women, who were later described as prostitutes. White men in the South had rallied, as they said, to the support of the honor of the abused white women. So aroused were southern whites by the accusations against the Scottsboro defendants that they hungered to lynch the black youths and thus accelerate the justice a trial would delay.

As I listened to Judge Carney's question, it occurred to me that the least I could do was protest in the name of the honor of black women. There was no suggestion in Judge Carney's condemnation that the "colored" woman involved was a prostitute, or that she suffered from anything other than her color.

I rose to do battle and walked quickly toward the bench, announcing as I approached that I was a member of the bar and an officer of the court. I asked if I might be heard on the question of the alleged infamy of living with what His Honor referred to as a "colored woman."

With my anger in full charge, as though daring the judge to hold me in contempt, and with reason thrown to the winds, I said, in as sarcastic a manner as I could manage, "Your Honor, perhaps I can offer you some survival techniques for living with what Your Honor has referred to as "a colored woman." I then added, "I believe I may have a bit more experience than Your Honor."

The courtroom became as silent as an underground vault, for I had spoken in a loud and insistent voice. It must have been commanding because court officers, trained to quell any such untoward interruption of court protocol, seemed stunned.

Judge Carney, however, only flushed. I had no way of knowing whether he was angry, or embarrassed at the sudden realization of what he had said. He was not abandoned by his sense of what to do. He invoked that saving grace available to all judges: he called a recess and disappeared through the door in back of his bench.

Immediately, I proceeded to the chambers of the chief justice, Irving Ben Cooper. I announced my mission to a woman at his reception desk. She seemed alarmed, and it occurred to me that she might be apprehensive about my anger. She remembered the rules, however, and asked if I had an appointment. When I said that I did not, she replied, predictably and with a straight face, that Judge Cooper was not in.

I then asked her to let him know my purpose. "Please tell him that it is extremely urgent that Bruce Wright see him about a matter of one of his judges making an offensive racist remark from the bench."

As she made notes, her fealty was betrayed by the one she sought to protect. The door in back of her opened, and the chief justice emerged. Taking me by surprise, he put one hand on my shoulder, as though in a fraternal rite. He seemed earnest and had the unflinching eye contact stressed by social workers.

He addressed me as though we were intimates. "Bruce, I know why you're here. There's nothing you can do about Judge Carney that's worse than what he's doing to himself. He's now in his chambers, practically flagellating himself."

I was struck by this reference to an ancient religious practice, but I suggested coldly that I would certainly do something worse. Before I could turn to leave, angrier than before because the judge had addressed me as "Bruce," as though I were a boy, he said, "Bruce, I'd like to come up and speak to the boys of the Harlem Lawyers Association sometime."

I suggested that he should perhaps get in touch with the president of the association, even as I would. It seemed that the Carney incident deserved an emergency meeting by that group. When I called the president, then Lawrence R. Bailey, he, too, was incensed. We agreed that the racism exhibited by Judge Carney disqualified him from being a judge in New York. Bailey instructed me to prepare a petition for filing with the appellate division of the state supreme court to seek a hearing in hope of removing Carney from the bench.

I prepared the petition in the belief that the Harlem Lawyer's Association finally had a valid issue that could justify its existence and emphasize something beyond the summer frivolity of a boat ride or its seasonal dance. It was also an opportunity to honor black women. I was soon to learn that my jesting family motto ("Things are never as bad as they seem; they are worse") would be realized in Afro-Saxon pomp.

A hot debate occurred over the Carney remark. The general feeling was that any protest by the association would affect the political careers of the members and nullify the ambitions of some to become judges or commissioners in the city or state governments. Several members contended that I was not a member of the association, that I was not in politics, that I was a radical and perhaps even a communist, and that the association should not risk its reputation and that of its membership simply because I wanted to press the matter. It was said that I had nothing to lose.

Sadly, neither did they. They failed to see that by remaining supine in face of such an insult, they might suffer the deprivation of the little they did have. They could not see that they were forfeiting respect by having none for their wives. They elected to do nothing.

A melancholy joke, offered to me as comfort, went that it was strange that the members of the association would not protest the honor of a "colored" woman because each of them was then living with a "colored" woman, either his own or someone else's wife.

Ultimately I persuaded the Harlem branch of the NAACP to seek the judge's removal. Judge Jonah Goldstein, who was about to retire from the Court of General Sessions, was appointed to preside over the hearing, and I was a witness. I was told that Judge Carney's lawyer was a close friend of Cardinal Spellman and very influential in the archdiocese.

Carney asserted, with some heat, that he did not have a discriminatory bone in his body, although he never denied uttering the words about the odium and incurable detriment of living with a "colored" woman. He recalled that when New York's first black judge, James S. Watson, was his colleague on the bench of the municipal court Carney had been the only white judge who would share a room with Watson at judicial conventions. That claim suggested a retroactive absolution and a prospective basis for being shriven of what he denied was a racist remark.

Finally, Carney's lawyer dictated a two-sentence letter of apology to the NAACP, not to the woman with whom the white defendant had been living. The apology was typed by Judge Goldstein's secretary. The lawyer read it and then placed it before Carney for his signature. He immediately signed it without reading it as though it was an order checked by a clerk for propriety.

I raised an objection, suggesting that the apology was that of the lawyer who had dictated it and certainly not that of Judge Carney. He stared at me icily through his rimless glasses and said, "You're trying to crucify me."

I assured him that although his sins were regarded as more scandalous than those of St. Augustine, I had no desire either to sanctify or deify him. At the time, Russell Crawford was president of the NAACP branch in Harlem. Despite my anger, he said, "We accept the apology." And that was the end of the matter.

I left in disgust, never dreaming that one day, I, too, would be a judge and the target of those who wished to have me drummed off the bench, as the PBA put it.

Shortly after his hearing, Carney was promoted to a higher bench. After I became a judge, whenever he and I accidentally shared the same elevator he habitually executed the Roman thumbs down gesture behind my back.

Other judges asked me, from time to time, why he did that. I could only reply that it was probably because he believed that I lived with a "colored" woman and therefore was beyond rehabilitation. Such remarks failed to win friends for me.

I never learned what happened to the poor white defendant who had become an unwitting victim of racist reaction because his emotional objectivity had allowed him to select a woman and she him, despite her nettlesome problem of being "colored."

For years, it was recently disclosed, neither affirmative action nor the laws against discrimination affected the Congress of the United States, which enacted so much civil rights legislation. Neither has the United States Supreme Court been affected by such legislation. Standing aloof, in analytical isolation, the court merely construes statutes and determines whether or not there is any taint of unconstitutional racism in their text or application.

Strangely enough, the rich and powerful law firms have long acted as though civil rights laws bear little or no application to them. And yet there has been not one famous lawsuit challenging the absence from such firms of Jews, blacks, and Hispanics. Most of the discrimination cases brought against law firms have been by women who allege sex discrimination. The excuses advanced for sex discrimination have in many ways rivalled the convoluted fictions invented to justify or explain prejudicial exclusions based on race.

My own position in the Proskauer firm was very unusual for those days. In 1950 the civil rights movement was unknown. For the most part, my stay there was a happy one and instructive. I left only because I saw no future for me there and neither did Bernard Lang, then the managing partner.

One Christmas Eve, as I worked late into the evening with Lang, he decided to take a break. He invited me into his office for a drink. I did not then drink, but of course did not reject the Scotch offered by a senior partner. He was then just completing a detail concerned with the acquisition and merger that came to be known as Federated Department Stores. "Bruce," he said, "I wonder how much it would take to pay us what we're really worth?"

Such a question was subject to both a flattering and its opposite interpretation. I smiled and said nothing. As the Scotch warmed my insides, I remembered that the young associates frequently talked about who could become a partner and when. I was curious about my own possibilities. I recalled the time when Bernard Baruch's brother, Simon, a former ambassador to the Hague, had marched me into Judge Proskauer's office, asking when I would be made a partner. Proskauer growled that he had nothing to do with making such decisions and he summarily dismissed us.

Remembering these events and aided by my drink, I decided it was an excellent time to ask about my prospects in the firm. I posed the question somewhat nervously, rather amazed that I could do so. Lang responded, "Bruce, let's talk about it at lunch on Monday, okay?" Naturally, I agreed.

The architecture and the stained glass at the Lawyers Club had a more pleasant meaning than the conversation at Monday's lunch. I had a Last Supper feeling in the midst of what seemed a money-changing cathedral. We discussed every conceivable subject except my future at the firm. Finally, as Lang was signing the chit, he said, "You know, Bruce, you've raised a rather important career question." He gave me an even look. "I can tell you right now that your chances of becoming a partner are nil. Our clients are not ready for it. However, you can remain with us as long as you like."

I was rebuffed but not terribly surprised, in the sense that surprise is totally unexpected and slashes at cherished visions. Not many whites ever said to a black luncheon guest, "*I'm* not ready for employment integration." It was always someone else who was not prepared for such a brave and radical experience. I liked to think that American color discriminations had hardened me and made me cynical and hard to surprise. But, the same idealistic hope that made me attribute such great expectations to the law always left some room for sharp surprise. I was not too attentive to the rest of the conversation. Already and irrevocably, I had decided that I would leave the comforts and discomforts of that firm. I had learned much.

The experience was not a total loss. I was then earning more money than my father had ever been paid. I went into private practice with three other young and relatively new lawyers. By 1968 I was working in the Lindsay Administration as counsel to the Human Resources Administration of the City of New York. The cry of black power had echoed throughout the country.

Many whites were so fearful and agitated that one would have thought that vengeful blacks, seeking to redress the wounds of slavery, had captured the secret of the world's most destructive nuclear weapons. A school strike was raging in Brooklyn. Blacks were making bitter charges of racism. Jewish teachers accused the black community of anti-Semitism. School decentralization was hotly debated, and the Ford Foundation was giving personnel and money to explore its possibilities.

Community control was the theme of the city's ghetto leaders.

Whites who could do so had either fled to the suburbs or placed their children in private or parochial schools. Public education in New York had suddenly become black and Hispanic.

Filled with visions of taking over the civil rights movement from its white directors, blacks demanded more black and Hispanic police officers. The emphasis was not so much on quotas as the need for more of everything.

7

Built-In Insensitivity

Instead of the beauty associated with color, its ability to in-spire and conjure up fantasies, dreams and joy, the *matter* of color seemed to pursue me like a demon. The perception of color seems to me a decisive force in human relations and in those that are dehumanizing.

The Jews speak of their Holocaust and the destruction of European Jewry. They weed that poisonous garden in poetry, prose, drama, the cinema, and melancholy conversation. They give artificial respiration to six million cadavers. Although they seem somewhat timid in condemning the disgraceful role of Pope Pius XII, their condemnation of an insane interlude of world history continues unabated. The condemnation should embrace Christendom and all who posed as faithful to that creed.

And yet America's dark servants, those graduates from slavery who became this country's poorly paid housekeepers, have had their repeated Kristall-nachts. Their blood has been wasted through an endurance of Christian hostility. A campaign of

173

terror has been a constant theme in black life, whether at the hands of justice or of the Ku Klux Klan.

The color holocaust has crippled millions of black lives in the polite manner of a "nice-slaveowner." Here, torture becomes a part of every day's limited existence. The headlines no longer advertise the American ethos by the details of a lynching: the lynching is covert, as in the form of a sniper firing from ambush.

Night-riding vigilantes are no longer fashionable. Volunteers in missions of vengeance now shoot from hidden places. The geography of such violence is no longer restricted to places in the rural South. It has moved to Buffalo, Boston and urban Atlanta. The nailing of testicles to a tree in Georgia has now become the removal of hearts from black victims in upstate New York.

The blacks perceive the mysterious ways of justice as they view courthouse consequences in Florida. Four police officers are acquitted of the charge of murdering a black man, despite the testimony of another officer who witnessed it all. In the subsequent riot, both blacks and whites are killed. The first conviction, however, is of a young black man for killing a white.

Whether justice triumphs in such a case becomes lost to blacks because they are the ones who are convicted whenever a white is killed. The situation becomes more complicated when a black is killed by a white.

Many blacks in the criminal justice system and in unrelated professions are bitterly amused by the white cry of "preferential treatment," "quotas," "affirmative action," and "reverse discrimination." These terms wage intellectual and ideological warfare against minority progress. Groups have surfaced demanding "white power," as though the locus of power had ever been with the blacks.

In some demonstrations, there have been signs proclaiming that "the niggers have too much." The blacks, once hunters of the constitutional dream, have now become the hunted, or, more correctly, remain the hunted. If it could ever be said that blacks had too much in terms of citizens' rights, it was because white society was used to its blacks having so little and because that meager measurement had been adopted as the standard.

Had whites been treated in America as the blacks have, I feel certain that they long ago would have undertaken either guerrilla warfare or prolonged civil disobedience for their rights. The American Revolution stands as precedent for how much white victims of oppression accept before they rebel. It is thus that the oppressed when liberated become the oppressors.

Judges, anxious to complete long calendars, believe they have no time for the exploration of learned theories that ask, "Why?" Perhaps considering the question of why suggests frightening answers by holding up a mirror to the history that created generations of burdens for today's Americans. For a proper analysis of that system, the harsh realities of color cannot be ignored.

Blacks, as slaves, were forbidden to learn to read or write. After emancipation, too large a segment of society sought to reinstate the bonds of slavery in methodical circumventions of freedom. The one-room shack, with all the amenities of a rural outhouse, sufficed for a black school in the South. The neighborhood concept of education for the young was cherished by and reserved for whites only.

For black children attending a segregated classroom, a bus ride of as many as a hundred miles a day was not unusual. On the way they had an opportunity to see gleaming, modern school buildings reserved for whites. Busing in those days was simply accepted as another fact of race separation. It was the rule for blacks and for the wealthy whites whose children were delivered to private schools. But as soon as busing was suggested as a device for integration and as a remedy for the shortcomings of the past, it became a national crime.

Once again, the cry of "Save the neighborhood" swept across the land. After all, whites had seceded from urban neighborhoods to flee black incursions. It did not make sense for them to

175

encourage or approve busing into their enclaves. To do so, they felt, would tarnish their mortgages and diminish their suburban isolation.

When blacks began to protest against civil service examinations based on long-existing and all-white educational values, the cry suddenly became "We want merit only." They did not mean merit for teaching and the education of blacks, which had been neglected for so many years. It was then a term that was only as flexible as it needed to be to bar black progress. With such democratic devices of "majority rule," the wonder is that it took blacks so long to express their resentment in violence and entry into the field of bank robberies and other "downtown" crimes.

The mention to my white colleagues of such surface historical references results in a dismissal of history and a pointing to the "advantages" of the present.

"Well," the comment generally goes, "whites have been poor, also, and they have not committed crimes in the same proportion as blacks."

Neither have blacks lynched whites, nor barred them from their churches, their swimming pools, their parks, schools, libraries, neighborhoods, and jobs. Nor have blacks allowed racial vengeance to dictate how they vote to decide a jury verdict. It appears to be otherwise among white jurors, especially when judging blacks or whites accused of killing blacks.

In 1977, I was questioning prospective witnesses for a lawsuit in which I was the plaintiff. I had sued the administrative judges of the court system, charging them and some district attorneys in New York with a conspiracy and a racist effort to deprive me of the same rights they accorded white judges and quiescent black judges. The Patrolmen's Benevolent Association was also a defendant in my federal litigation.

A jury clerk in the Bronx drew me aside and handed me a sheet of paper from a yellow legal pad. It was the jottings of the foreman of an all-white jury then hearing a case against a black defendant. It had been left in the jury room after the panel had been ushered back into the courtroom.

The notations were disjunctive but nevertheless wholly concerned with a "nigger" fixation. Some excerpts will illustrate the point.

"All niggers have guns," it began. "We should have Russian justice here, that is, just shoot the bastards. Well, we've got to give this nigger a fair trial. Hope the judge likes niggers."

It is not that the judge must have affection for blacks, nor is it necessary for jurors to have such a tender emotion. The difficulty is in bringing objectivity and impartiality to a jury in a race-stricken land. It seems inescapable that white judges reach conclusions that reflect white community standards.

Most people regard the police as the first line of protection against criminals. Because so many blacks are arrested and charged with criminal conduct, white society normally sides with police and tends to regard officers in the heroic image those guardians project of the themselves. The outrage is spoken loudly in the black residential areas of New York every time a white officer is acquitted when charged with killing a black. Such acquittals confirm the oft-repeated belief that no white officer will ever be convicted for shooting a black.

Jury verdicts have borne out that view as a fatal statistic. In 1973, Clifford Glover was shot and killed by a white officer named Thomas Shea. When tried for that killing, Shea said, in addition to expressing the belief that he was in danger, that he thought the ten-year-old was an adult robbery suspect.

Although this offered little excuse for shooting to kill, it did offer some commentary on the quality of the defense a policeman could make with confidence in a murder case.

When Shea was asked if he could not tell the difference between a little boy of ten and a fully grown man, especially at a distance of just three feet, he replied, "All I saw was the color of his skin." Thus did he express an oath of fealty to the nation's color ethic.

I believed at the time that such an explicitly public confession so solemnly sworn would not only condemn Shea but also reveal Police Department policy for what it was, is, and always has been. I innocently believed that the jury would convict for such a wanton killing, based, as Shea had said, on the only thing he had seen, the color of the little boy's skin.

I was wrong, of course. He was acquitted. It brought little satisfaction to Glover's mother that the Police Department was so embarrassed by Shea's public display of police feeling and contempt for black skin that it dismissed him. It was a curious circumstance to some that the department appeared to prosecute his dismissal with much more zeal than that used by the Queens County district attorney in pressing the charge of murder against Shea.

That Shea could confess openly his animus against dark skin color and still win acquittal is a melancholy comment on the cheapness of black life and the power of propaganda.

The killing of Randy Evans shortly after that of Glover introduced a new police defense. Novel and apparently effective. Torsney, a white officer, simply walked up to Evans and put a bullet in his head. Evans, a teenager, was doing nothing but standing near where he lived. Torsney claimed that an attack by a rare form of epilepsy made him do it. He too, was acquitted.

With so much black-on-black crime, one would tend to think that even blacks regard black life as cheap and as worthless as does white society. It has been said that blacks are not held to such a strict and rigorous standard of accountability when they are in conflict with other blacks.

One judge is reported to have said, regarding a case in which a black defendant was acquitted and his accuser was also black, "If this [the accuser] had been a white man, the black man would have been convicted. Negroes in cases of this type receive more than equal rights; juries seem to think it's okay for them to cut, if it's another colored person that is cut."

The hard fact is that, all too often, a black is *rewarded* with a minimal rap on the wrist for harming another black. But if a black harms or deprives a white, the judicial whip lashes out at him.

Pretty much the same conclusion was reached in a 1966 study done by Harry Kalven and Hans Zeisel on the subject of how racist influences affect both judges and jurors in America. It was there demonstrated, if any demonstration was needed, that many jurors refuse to divorce themselves from the racism and prejudice that are a part of their everyday existence.

One white juror, among the many interviewed for the study, put into perspective the general feelings expressed by most, when he spoke of his judgment of a black defendant: "Niggers have to be taught to behave. I feel that if he hadn't done that, he'd probably done something else probably even worse and that he should be put out of the way for a good long while."

Private vengeance brought to public judgment may be found in a distressing and melancholy pageant acted out before my eyes in the New York City Criminal Court. It was 1970. At the time, I was new on the bench and simply observing what went on in the courtrooms of the experienced judges.

I sat on a front row bench, hoping to learn something. In a striking example of the urgency with which the police arrest black men, I saw an enormous black man standing beside the defense counsel before the bench. His Afro hairdo was in a state of disarray. He stared straight ahead, wearing the expression of a fierce stoic.

It was a cold February day, but he wore no shoes. His only clothing was trousers and a soiled and flimsy undershirt. He could have been a statute. He was a breathing still life. His presence suggested to me the image of an African chief captured by slavers. To his right, at a table reserved for the district attorney, sat a man barely recognizable as white.

He was swathed in bandages from head to toe. One arm was in a sling. The other arm had a cane crooked over it. He remained seated, I imagined, because of his wounded condition.

The white judge, an excitable man of some years, seemed deeply moved by the *pietism* of the bandaged victim. He rose to his feet and leaned over the end of the bench and asked, "My God, man, what happened to you?"

The man lifted his cane weakly, and it trembled as he pointed at the black defendant. He was a speaking mummy. "He cut me, your Honor," he replied. His voice sounded as though it rasped from a distant echo chamber.

In an extraordinary example of contempt for the presumption of innocence, the judge moved swiftly to the other side of the bench and asked sternly of the black man, "Why did you cut him that way?"

Before his lawyer could intervene, and without a second's hesitation, the defendant answered, "He called me a black nigger, that's why." He continued to stare straight ahead, now with a trace of anger and defiance on his face.

The judge, reaching for that wisdom which mythology says is inseparable from the task of judging, shook his head from side to side, remonstrating, "But don't you know that when he heals and sees his scars every morning when he shaves, he's going to call you the same thing?"

This colloquy was ended suddenly when the black man said tersely, and with some heat, "I better not hear the motherfucker."

There was instant clapping and laughter from the blacks in the courtroom.

It was not at all humorous. It was the tragedy of one revolutionary standing alone; a single rebel against forces that victimized millions of others; the classical symmetry of the victim aiding and abetting his own defeat. I felt, also, that the judge himself had defeated justice. I hoped I would never be that kind of judge.

How has America changed since the abolition of slavery? The question, of course, is addressed to the country's politics of sociology. It has to be admitted that conditions differ from those of the days of Dred Scott, when that slave had to sue to have determined the question of whether or not he had a right to sue to have determined the question of whether or not he had a right to sue.

The judicial system has been altered in some ways. It has been faithful to the precept of reluctant change and, like Dowson's lover of Cynara, after its fashion. The nine competing opinions of the United States Supreme Court, in the case of *Furman v. Georgia,* allowed five of the justices to offer a fleeting solace that the death penalty was unconstitutional. But it was left to Justice Thurgood Marshall to write that it is discriminatorily applied against the poor and members of minority groups, not to mention against men and women. Ethel Rosenberg, of course, is an exception. In her execution and that of her husband can be discovered entire areas of judicial discrimination having nothing to do with color but everything to do with American anti-Semitism. Mr. Justice Douglas also agreed that the penalty should be abolished if it discriminates against one by "reason of his race, religion, wealth, social position or class" and if imposed under circumstances that allow room "for the play of such prejudices."

Douglas was consistent in the *Furman* case with his prior dissent in *Francis v. Resweber*. There, a young black man, Willie Francis, had been sentenced to death. After "difficult preparation for execution," the executioner pulled the switch and a current of electricity surged through the boy's body, intended to cause his death. But the chair had malfunctioned and young Francis did not die. The state of Louisiana repaired both Francis

181

and the chair and the authorities readied the death chambers once again to carry out the execution. Lawyers intervened, claiming that the Eight Amendment to the Constitution barred a second experience in the chair because it would be cruel and unusual punishment.

When the case came to the Supreme Court, Douglas dissented. The majority held, in effect, that Francis had been sentenced to death, that he had not died, and that it would not offend the Constitution to carry out the death sentence. It is a unique case. It has happened only to a black person. The case has excited scholarly law review comment and one author is completing a book about Willie Francis. While I am not at liberty to reveal what the author's research uncovered, it can be said that the conclusion is that Francis was the victim of a monstrous frame-up.

One of the most powerful arguments against the death penalty is that sometimes irreversible mistakes are made and the wrong person is executed.

At a recent conference in Washington on minority problems and criminal justice, a Japanese-American federal judge recalled his childhood days in an American concentration camp. That the Supreme Court referred to those camps as "relocation centers" did not ease the harsh fact that American citizens of Japanese ancestry were summarily uprooted and forcefully evacuated from the West Coast shortly after Pearl Harbor was bombed.

No presumption of innocence protected them. They were treated as criminals, although no criminal charges were filed. The government announced that it had reasonable ground to act to prevent sabotage and espionage.

Mr. Justice Douglas did not file a dissent in those cases, much to the distress of those of us who looked on him as a lonely conscience of the Court during World War II. One was left to wonder if his youth on the West Coast had somehow affected his view of Americans of Japanese ancestry.

He reached his *Furman* views on the death penalty circuitously through the *Rosenberg* case. Although in *Rosenberg* the Supreme Court had declined to review the death sentence, subsequent writs were presented the Court in an effort to bar the execution of Julius and Ethel Rosenberg. They had been convicted of espionage under a 1917 statute. But a few days before their execution, Douglas had issued a stay. The full Court, in an extraordinary summer session, vacated it, and the Rosenbergs were put to death several hours later. It was then that Douglas filed his dissent urging that they not be executed.

We now know from a book by James F. Simon that some of Douglas's colleagues disapproved of the stay and dissent, believing he had given both simply for the publicity value.

The records of the Supreme Court reveal that Douglas had voted to deny review of the Rosenberg case on five separate occasions. I had always viewed the refusal of the high court to review the Rosenberg appeal as the last act in a ritual sacrifice of human beings to the god of anti-Semitism as reflected during the McCarthy era in America. That there was a Jewish judge and a Jewish prosecutor does nothing to modify the intensity of national emotion generated by the Rosenberg trial.

Rabbi Wise and Cardinal Spellman joined in a widely publicized effort to abate some of the anti-Semitism of the time. A young Jewish volunteer for the army was found and he took his oath on the steps of City Hall with great fanfare and notice. Trained and shipped to Korea, he was predictably killed. While many recall the Rosenbergs, few remember the young Jewish man and the desperate rituals that led to his death.

Such things need to be mentioned because Jews are a minority, albeit a white one, in American society, and I have long classified them with blacks as an endangered species in a Christian society.

That my Jewish friends do not share this vision of right-wing and conservative sway in American life and the jeopardy it suggests does not lessen its impact on me. Nor is it pleasant to see how many American Jews themselves have become a part of the conservative census.

In Mr. Justice Frankfurter it was known as "judicial restraint," a surprising attitude for a man who had been such an activist that he was prominent in the celebrated Sacco and Vanzetti Defense Committee. Although he could vote to reverse the Mississippi conviction of "a poor devil of a young Negro lad," he could exhibit another, aloof side.

He voted, for example, against allowing the law clerks of the justices to have a Christmas party in the courthouse, to which "colored messengers" would be invited.

On a national basis, apart from the civil rights movement and its Jewish heroes and heroines, the lean toward conservatism appears to have been led by the American Jewish Committee. Ironically, the push in that direction seems to have begun in the midst of the libertarian 1960s.

In 1963, *Commentary*, the official publication of the committee, published as its lead article an essay entitled "My Negro Problem and Yours." In that long and rambling piece, Norman Podhoretz, *Commentary*'s editor, reviewed his troubled relationship with black youngsters in the Brooklyn neighborhood of his youth.

While proclaiming that the "wholesale merging of the two races is the most desirable" through assimilation and, "let the brutal word come out, miscegenation," he nevertheless realized that he would not want his daughter "to marry one." Since that time *Commentary* has had a succession of articles clinging to middle-American conservatism on the country's ethnic dilemma.

Commentary has adopted black Thomas Sowell as its resident Afro-Saxon. In the stodginess of his views on blacks and his condemnation of them for relying, as many do, on welfare contributions and federal antipoverty programs, he emerges as an arch-conservative.

In allying himself with the enemies of black progress through government-sponsored social programs, he seems to be ashamed of his blackness, but without it he would not be the useful favorite son and dark pamphleteer he now is for the views of *Commentary*. One of his 1978 essays is titled with the question: "Are Quotas Good for Blacks?"

Earlier, in another edition of the magazine, Midge Decter had delivered a harsh polemic titled "Looting and Liberal Racism." She did not think the looters during the New York City blackout of 1977 should be referred to as "animals." She preferred "scurrying urban insect life" to the imagery of the jungle. Apparently she wished to keep comparison as close as she possibly could to the roaches that infest poor neighborhoods.

In 1978, Joseph Adleson took to the pages of *Commentary* to write his opposition to living with quotas. He felt that any concept of quotas in education was a deception for "marginal" or "unqualified" minorities and that their promotion would be a corruption both of language and conduct.

It reminded me of a dinner in the luxurious suburb of Rye, New York, at which I was the black guest. I sat next to a teacher who had taught at Hunter College High School. She bemoaned what she called the misdirected power of the black students there in persuading the school system to teach Swahili. She shook her head as she said, "This year, we'll teach Swahili. Next semester we'll teach remedial Swahili." In the best *Commentary* tradition, she presented a stunning example of the social and intellectual contempt reserved for black studies and ambition.

In 1976, Michael Novak's *Commentary* contribution had been titled "Race and Truth." He emphasized that "job quotas, charity, subsidies, preferential treatment tend to undermine self-reliance and pride of achievement." Other articles in the 1970s have covered such issues as "Western guilt and Third World poverty" (P. T. Bauer) and the *De Funis* and *Baake* cases, which went to the Supreme Court. The magazine's thematic bete noire has been Kenneth Clark, with Andrew Young as a late contender for that title.

It is almost as though *Commentary*'s conservative argument against black goals has had some effect and influence on white judges and their regard for the large number of blacks who appear before them. And so there has been change in the atmosphere of America. It is not the change that was hoped for as a result of the egalitarian activities in the 1960s. That decade is but a memory now, and the affectionate alliance between Jews and blacks seems as distant as another planet. Conditions for black lawyers as well have changed little. Perhaps they can now feel better when entering most courthouses, almost as though they have someone there they know, or know about.

There are now some black judges and clerks in almost every courthouse in New York City and in most of the other large cities of the country. They are there by virtue of a quota system that differs from the one the enemies of quotas are anxious to nullify.

Either by deliberation or inadvertence, blacks are severely restricted in their ambition to become judges. Most often, when election time comes around, the black politicians may be given a quota of one judge for the supreme court or the civil court. Black lawyers are still regarded with suspicion, as though they do not meet white standards. There are implicit insults even in remarks meant as compliments.

My own work product has been described as excellent by critical clerks, but only because I was once associated with a white law firm. They would not say I was hired because of my preparation.

Whites have an historical insensitivity that makes them remote and aloof from the depleting significance of being black in

America or in South Africa. Although the two apartheids can be distinguished, they are nonetheless generically linked. Both rely on attitudes, rewards, and deprivations derived from theories of racial superiority on the one hand and racial inferiority on the other.

Judges, both black and white, reared and living in New York City, have all too often revealed themselves as seemingly unaware of the insults built into such a system and way of life. Long before FM became popular, or even existed, the one non-commercial radio station that broadcast daily and evening programs of classical music was the city's own WNYC. Its distinguished director for so many years was Seymour Siegel. In addition to the "Sunrise Symphony," there were programs of folk songs and jazz. One day, to my amazement, I heard some "darky" songs being sung. The composer was Stephen Foster.

As a black taxpayer, it occurred to me that I did not have to tolerate racist antebellum hymns to the happiness of slavery on publicly owned radio. I therefore began a protest dialogue with Siegel. He was understanding and assured me that no such lyrics would be sung on that station in the future. They were played again, of course, by a rebellious all-white staff, who accused me of being a book-burner and a latter-day Nazi.

During the 1950s the New York City Housing Authority began construction of a low-rent development in the midst of Harlem. A large sign advertised its name: the Stephen Foster Houses. I addressed a protest to the chairman of the authority, pointing out the insult to Harlem's black citizens implicit in a housing monument to the memory of Foster.

The chairman, although unable to see anything insulting to blacks, referred me to the member of the authority responsible for naming the project. That member was Frank Crosswaith, a black man, famous in Harlem as one of the founders of the Harlem Labor Union.

Exchanging correspondence with him confirmed once again

that insensitivity and the tacit racial insult escapes the notice of some blacks as well as whites. His letter to me was brief and biting. It said: "Dear Sir: I do not often respond to crank letters. However, you should know that the songs of Stephen Foster prepared the North for the migration of the Negro."

I could not resist responding and I asked him what such songs did for those Negroes who remained in the South, assuming that his first statement had any validity. He did not reply.

Crosswaith then turned over the entire correspondence to George Schuyler, then the New York editor of the *Pittsburgh Courier*, a black weekly newspaper. One of my points had been that Foster had been a native of Pittsburgh and not a New Yorker or a resident of Harlem. Schuyler, who had married a white Texan, was a man of impressive brilliance and imagination. His daughter Philippa was a genius and a recognized concert pianist.

In the late 1920s, Schuyler had published a bitterly satirical novel entitled *Black No More*. Described at one point as a "black Mencken," he became progressively more conservative and was sometimes referred to as Harlem's Westbrook Pegler. It was even rumored that he was Harlem's only member of the John Birch Society.

Schuyler was fiercely loyal to Frank Crosswaith. One edition of the *Pittsburgh Courier* carried a headline shouting, "Harlem Lawyer Attacks Crosswaith." In an editorial, he then admonished me for what he called "racial immaturity." He lived long enough to be distressed by seeing the Stephen Foster Houses changed to the Malcolm X Houses through the efforts of their black and Hispanic residents.

If the racial atmosphere in America is ever to be improved, the blacks who are called leaders must offer genuine leadership. They cannot simply be the tools of the white establishment, for such leadership is ersatz and calculated to keep the anger of the blacks internal and tranquilized.

It is the kind of leadership that was paraded through the ghetto of Miami during a racial disturbance, using loudspeakers to tell the blacks to count their American blessings and to go home and trust the very systems of justice that caused rioting in the first place.

Such leadership obeys a directed policy but does not make policy. Genuine black leadership must be muscular and not swayed by those who would neutralize it into puppetry. It must address publicly and express exactly what most blacks really think and feel about white American society and why.

Passive acceptance of racism merely fertilizes the roots of that oppression and aids its growth. But from the ranks of quiet, well-dressed lawyers come our judges of all colors. They are the respectable members of society who have accepted the American way of brutal death. The American way of life has touched exposed nerves by its racism not only among blacks, but among Hispanics of color, and Jews as well.

The Jews, who are considered white, have built up through the years great and powerful blocs, such as B'nai B'rith and the Anti-Defamation League. Their publications are widely read, and their whiteness has allowed them to have white options and opportunities. Many have acquired great wealth.

This is not to say that all Jews were always wealthy, or are wealthy today. I long ago read Michael Gold's *Jews Without Money* and have known many Jews who have struggled through poverty. Nor did I have to read about *Fortune*'s five hundred greatest corporations to know that the wealth of America is primarily in the hands of the white Protestant establishment, which controls the banks, property, and government. The judiciary has been tainted by anti-Semitism, as well as by the racism that has color as its focus.

The History of the American Bar by Charles Warren of the Boston bar has an index that reads like the names in the purest Protestant social register, except for its inclusion of the name of

Judah Benjamin. The Association of the Bar of New York, which passes judgment on those selected for the bench in New York City, refused to admit Jews for many years and for even longer would not consider blacks. *Jurisprudence in Action,* however, published by the association in 1953, does not mention such discrimination.

This aspect of the association is also ignored in *Causes and Conflicts,* the centennial history of that body, which dates from 1860. The suppression of black and Jewish membership in former years only exceeds the suppression of any mention of those scandals in a so-called learned profession.

In 1949, New York, despite its large number of Jewish lawyers, had yet to have a surrogate who was Jewish. The Republicans nominated George Frankenthaler. He became the first Republican and the first member of the Jewish faith ever elected to the surrogate's court since its creation in 1880.

Louis Jaffe, of the Proskauer firm, had suggested that I work in that campaign, and I performed minor telephone functions for the Frankenthaler headquarters. There I was able to see the great volume of anti-Semitic mail that arrived daily. Most of it was anonymous, and it italicized some of the strong underground feelings against Jews. It seemed to make little difference that Frankenthaler was by far the best qualified of those contesting for the office. He won by only 1,150 votes.

This anti-Semitism reflected a renaissance in local neo-Nazi thinking in New York. The fear and bias outstripped in their vituperation anything that I received during my years on the Criminal Court. Letters to me expressed a racist contempt but no fear. The general theme was that I should "go back to Africa and learn from the apes."

One person enrolled me as a subscriber to every conceivable publication. This more impersonal annoyance resulted in my membership in book clubs, the large-print *New York Times* for the blind, the National Association, various mutual funds, and the National Rifle Association. Calls came to my chambers daily in response to "your inquiry" about an eclectic catalog of merchandise, both practical and erotic. One dismayed resident of an East Side cooperative came to my chambers personally to leave a prospectus and an invitation for me to invade the restrictive covenants of Park Avenue's territorial imperative.

That so many white judges are either unaware or insensitive to the degradations that are routine for blacks does not astonish me as much as it used to. What does cause concern is that self-appointed liberals and moderates often exhibit the same ignorance.

My two oldest sons went through the Ethical Culture educational system and its Fieldston School in Riverdale. On one Father's Day at Fieldston, sitting next to Eli Wallach, I was amazed to see and hear tthe music instructors leading fathers and sons in a series of "darky" songs.

It was my unhappy duty to interrupt that ethnic harmony with an objection that stopped the singing at least until I made my angry departure. When my oldest son was five years old, he came home one afternoon and began turning circles. Afraid that he might become dizzy and hurt himself, I asked him what he was doing. He replied, "Turning to butter."

Furious because I recognized at once the *Little Black Sambo* source of that symbolism, I asked him where he had learned it. Predictably, he said that his teacher had not only read the story to his class but had assigned roles for acting it out.

When I protested the exposure of uncritical minds to what has become a racial stereotype, I was once again called a book-burner. I was referred to the school's psychologist.

In my anger, I told her that unless that book awaited a more mature and critical class of students, I would remove my son from the school. She said that my anger prevented a cool, rational, and analytical discussion of the problem and that perhaps we should schedule another conference after she returned from a visit to New England, where she was going to see the changing colors of the leaves in autumn. I sought to assure her that she need not go so far as New England if it was color she was interested in.

It became evident that it was going to be extremely difficult, if not impossible, to have a meaningful discussion with her. A problem of race and color seemed of less concern to her than her personal urgency to see the colors of autumn leaves in a distant place.

The more I insisted that *Little Black Sambo* presented certain dangers for uncritical minds, the more she stressed the dangers of being called a book-burner and a censor. She seemed to have no interest in the authorities on early education I cited and the documentation with which I supported my protest.

She smiled tolerantly when I asked her to look at the materials I had assembled on the subject of how racist influence can taint young minds with harmful stereotypes such as the *Sambo* illustrations. The interview was futile.

I deteriorated into abuse. She seemed baffled when I asked her if her preoccupation with trees had ever allowed her to think about how many blacks had been lynched on her bearers of beautiful colors. She said that that was hardly relevant to our discussion, which then ended abruptly.

My worst fears were realized when my son, Geoff, then all of four years old, was referred to as "Sambo" by his closest little white friend at school. It seemed useless to revive further discussion with the psychologist simply to say to her, "I told you so."

It is always difficult to persuade those who believe themselves to be liberals, as well as those middle-of-the-roaders who like to call themselves moderates, that, all too often, they may not live up to the hopeful adjectives they use to describe themselves. Such descriptions, of course, spring from the morality of self-interest and, perhaps, some degree of self-doubt.

Built-In Insensitivity

P. Jay Sidney, an actor and a selfless activist, has long been an analyst of the little tragedies that give the human comedy so much depth. In particular, he detests those whites who piously but ambiguously describe themselves as moderates. To stress his contempt for what he called "mugwumpery," he will always ask such confessors of their own status if they would wish their wives to be "moderately" virtuous. Of course, the danger in the universal application of such a question is that it might have to be altered just a bit, depending upon the gender of the confessor. So-called moderate Americans are not always male, or, if so, always married.

Patriotic white studies are the foundation of America's educational experience, especially in history. White America expected blacks to be as deliriously emotional about the Bicentennial as anyone else, even though the only thing blacks would rationally celebrate dating back to two hundred years would be their miraculous survival of Christian bondage.

Adopting George Washington as the father of my country would mean neglecting his Mount Vernon colony slaves. My white colleagues on the bench failed to understand my feelings about majority rule and my necessary exclusion from some aspects of the American celebration. They refused to follow my assumptions. And yet, these are the same reasoners who expect black urban peasants to stop and analyze the blessings of American apartheid before rioting in the streets or burning symbols of black oppression.

What they also ignore is that the angry underclass that takes to the streets regards the black bourgeoisie as aloof elitists who serve as the dark agents of white oppression. In many ways, the destructive uprisings of poor blacks have resulted in the dwarf step progress enjoyed by those minorities with token symbols of advanced employment.

There is a grass-roots apprehension and understanding of reality, which makes ordinary people of the streets wary of blacks who are placed in certain positions. Jawn Sandifer, was, at one time, the black deputy assistant administrative judge in charge of the criminal branches of the supreme court and of the criminal courts in New York City. He is regarded with bitter suspicion by minorities who look at the criminal justice system. It is suspected that he was placed in his position to show how liberal the system is.

In keeping the system functioning, he became just another one of the judges supervising the warehousing of as many blacks and Hispanics as possible. His role in having me transferred from the Criminal to the Civil Court in 1974, as a disciplinary measure to appease the police, has been described as highly suspect.

When I was returned to the Criminal Court in 1978, it is believed to have been a gesture to avoid embarrassing examinations before the trial of Sandifer and Charles Breitel, then chief judge of New York's Court of Appeals. My federal lawsuit against the administrative judges and others was then pending and earlier depositions had revealed some strange inconsistencies in the various official versions of my precipitate transfer.

The small number of black judges have found it an advantage to their outward state of aloof serenity not to jeopardize their membership in the society of judges. To be outspoken and critical is to risk nettlesome assignments and to forego any opportunity for promotion.

A black Criminal Court judge does well to heed Mayor Koch's warning that those who do not reflect by their conduct his own inflexible attitudes toward judging need not expect reappointment. Accused of racism because of his notable lack of enthusiasm for black appointments, Koch has little fear of black reaction. Blacks do not vote in great numbers and are thus regarded as political eunuchs.

Even judges who will not risk saying so publicly would like to see themselves as members of an independent judiciary. Privately, they express resentment of a mayor who wishes them to pay strict allegiance to his whim and his own purely political and opportunist view of justice. They do not wish to be puppets for such a mayor's expedient ventriloquism. And yet, by not making a public outcry, they become the very puppets they wish to condemn. I would like to see the training of potential judges begin at the college level. Before anyone could become eligible for law school, whether or not he or she wished to opt for the ambition of judging, each should be required to study some of the more suppressed aspects of American history, including the terror and subjugation and bending of the spirit in modern society caused by black slavery under the Constitution. The curriculum would include a study of the role of the law in making slavery legal for so long and the influence of such bondage in shaping the attitudes of blacks and their limited participation in American life.

Such students, whether white or black or other, would be exposed to an analysis of the peculiar sociology of inner-city and urban existence and the conspiracies of reality, overt or otherwise, that have restricted and limited black ambition and options.

Coupled with such studies would be emphasis on black heroes in history, black American patriots, black inventors, and black family life, about which students in particular are woefully ignorant. Many blacks, as well as whites, have no knowledge whatsoever of these things. They, too, should learn.

No person called upon to judge the residents of a society so long scorned and held up to contempt because of color stereotypes deeply ingrained in American thinking and emotions should dare come to the bench as ignorant of the black circumstance as most now are. Absent such instruction, blacks and other aliens to America's society become no more than detested grist for the country's judicial mills. Such an education might well be revealing and beneficial. It would at least be a significant departure from the white studies and historical platitudes that

195

allow students to see no warts on America's white figures and no significant black individuals at all. Absent such teaching, typical American education at all levels becomes no more than a perpetuation of a class system that the Constitution's libertarian language denies as a matter of practice in theory only.

In a society shriven of black bondage, the residual trappings of such an antebellum culture should also be rooted out. That can never happen in America as long as law students are taught merely the techniques of analyzing the complex facts of commercial situations. The current tradition is to teach them tactics and ways to affect legislation which will not jeopardize the institutions they hope to join as perpetuators of policy. Such political inbreeding does not bring about social change that would dramatize the Constitution's meaning of even-handed justice for all, no matter what a citizen's skin color.

Such instruction has been called sociological jurisprudence by Roscoe Pound, once the dean of the Harvard Law School. That theory would seek to make lawyers and judges more than impersonal calculators summing up the historical bias of the society in which they are aloof agents.

Pound more than any other scholar of the law sought to emphasize humane realism and the incorporation of social studies into the law school curriculum. He recognized the powerful influence of law and lawyers in society and their role in national and local government. The law, he thought, could be the promissory device for achieving social reconstruction in American life.

Pound urged a movement that would put the human factor in a central place and would reject the emotional logic of the past, the agrarian and evangelical confusions that made so many accept both their God and the enslavement of others at the same time. He seemed to differ sharply with Oliver Wendell Holmes, who did not like the idea of experimenting with the Fourteenth

Amendment. And yet, it was precisely that amendment which called for a national experiment.

It was indeed a radical concept to provide "equal protection of the laws" for the emancipated blacks who had only recently been adopted as citizens and persons. The Fourteenth Amendment had become an instrument for social engineering, although, as it developed, a much-neglected one in confirming the privileges and immunities of black citizens.

No judge who presides over the tensions and the violence of alienation and condemnation should ever dare to sit in judgment of those dark strangers to his or her way of life. Ironically, in terms of the teachings of history, an American judge can feel that he has more in common with a white Russian than with a black American.

As society swings into an era of rightist conservatism, it becomes less and less likely that the law will lead to social experimentation, either under the Fourteenth Amendment or otherwise. Neither does the American mood seem receptive to the proposed Equal Rights Amendment to promote the interests of women, whose plight is so often identified with that of blacks in American society.

When Pablo Neruda addressed the P.E.N. Club after he had won his Nobel Prize, he said that the blacks are the luckless race. He could have added that women are the luckless sex.

The occasional weekend retreats, now provided for judges by the Office of Court Administration, do not engage the hard questions that burden the everyday business of criminal courts in cities with large black and Hispanic populations. Thus far, many writers on the subject of racial discrimination in the courts have done no more than deplore what exists.

Former federal judge Marvin Frankel has written an extremely useful little book called *Criminal Sentences*. He subtitles it *Law without Order*. Frankel notes the great disparity between sentences imposed on blacks and the poor as compared with those for identical crimes imposed on whites. And even when the crimes are not the same, there are remarkable distinctions.

Irving Ben Cooper is a federal judge in New York whose confirmation by the Senate was fraught with controversy. Competing views were expressed concerning his emotional stability. He was the chief judge of the Court of Special Sessions when I asked that Judge George Carney be removed because of his expressed views about a "colored" woman.

In January 1980, I appeared in his court to move the admission of John Sheehan as a member of the federal bar. It appeared that Judge Cooper had lost his notes. While a large number of lawyers waited to have their admissions moved, he seemed to be searching among the papers on the bench, talking all the while. Among the young lawyers awaiting admission were several Asians. Judge Cooper selected that occasion to tell a Chinese accent joke.

Earlier in his career on the federal bench, Cooper had been called upon to sentence two defendants, one white, one black. The white defendant was a former Wall Street broker. He had been convicted of illegally selling stocks. He had collected a commission of some $250,000, which he laundered through a secret Swiss bank account. He had perjured himself before the federal grand jury that investigated him.

Judge Cooper remarked that the well-dressed defendant was not likely to repeat such an act. He fined him some $90,000 and placed him on probation for a year. Simple subtraction may reveal that, in that case at least, crime did pay. When Judge Cooper sentenced the black man, however, prison was on his mind. The black man, the sole supporter of a diabetic wife and daughter, was a truck driver. He had been convicted of stealing a television set from the truck he drove. It was a black-and-white set worth less than $100. The judge sent him to jail for a year.

The act may have been society's vengeance, but it was also society's folly. The black man's wife became a ward of welfare. One can only speculate on the problems the husband has had since his release while seeking employment.

And so the improvement of the criminal justice system, quite apart from its racism, should appeal to those who perceive how the taxpayers' money is wasted in some instances. As for improving the quality of justice in the criminal courts, again, that depends upon the judges and their understanding.

This, as noted, is a matter of preparation. Until society is prepared to educate its judges *before* they ascend the bench, little change in the system can be expected. This means that, to a large extent, racism will continue unabated. Little else can be expected in a country still torn by school desegregation lawsuits, employment problems, and bitter and angry challenges to what used to be called affirmative action. Also continued will be the repressive quotas reserved for blacks in all areas of life, quotas of limitation, which majority rule seems not to oppose.

The opinion held of Lyndon B. Johnson by those who shape the nation's attitudes and thoughts does not appear flattering. He was perceived as Machiavellian, given to political duplicity and maneuvering. Nevertheless, he was more useful to the cause of blacks in America than any other president. His unprecedented linking of arms with blacks on the campus at Howard University while singing "We Shall Overcome" was a gesture of incredible goodwill from the White House for the black struggle.

It is such emotional involvement that offers comfort to black citizens of the United States. Johnson was the only president to display such a public identification with black ambition for survival. His was the first acknowledgment from the fountainhead of American power that blacks and whites enjoyed national kinship. It gave blacks all over the country a tremendous emotional boost. I doubt that it did anything to abate black crime, however.

199

The nomadic black and urban peasants who wander the streets, engaging in crimes which they believe aid their survival, seldom read of presidential news conferences or executive sing-ins. For those of us who relished the idea of a president suggesting in lyrics that the dark underclass should overcome, it was incredible. It seems doubtful that such a romantic gesture will ever be repeated. Certainly, President Ronald Reagan's attitudes point in the opposite direction from interracial good will.

The brief Johnson era of good feeling is all but forgotten now. It is a nostalgic footnote to a time that has disappeared, swallowed up by another and different era. Society remembers the murders, the rapes, the robberies, and the muggings attributed to blacks. Few recall that some fifteen black children disappeared in Atlanta and that now and then a corpse was discovered.

No headlines blaze across the front pages of the tabloids, however, when blacks are discovered to be murdered with their hearts cut out. This symbol of racial hate becomes intensified when it is remembered how complicated and time-consuming it is for expert surgeons to cut out a human heart. The bone of the sternum must be sawed through. The heart is protected behind the rib cage in the depths of the upper body. That racial hate is able to compel one to such lengths is a source of wonderment. It makes one ask if there is anything in America that will cure the wound of race, whether it be a university that trains citizens to be judges or some other remedy.

Alexis de Tocqueville visited America in the 1830s to see how democracy was faring in the then new republic. He remarked that the bench and the bar were America's nobility. Although he mentioned that Americans were willing to sue over any conceivable injustice, he did not explore theories of justice. The law, not justice, is emphasized.

Law and order were the twin cries of Adolf Hitler at one time.

Hitler's Final Solution for the Jews proved, if any proof was needed, that all too often law has little or nothing to do with justice. And "law and order" is the cry heard throughout America today. Politicians win elections by standing in the jailhouse door in their commercials, promising that that is where they will excommunicate all criminals.

The more the politicians threaten to stop crime and imprison criminals, the more crime we have. The newspapers never fail to describe a black defendant as such. Seldom if ever is a white defendant so described. Given the prevailing climate of thought, or reaction, on the subject, most people will assume one charged with crime is black.

None of this should be read as a defense of black criminals or their crimes. What to do about crime and criminals is the imponderable that confronts both me and the system. It is clear that prisons have not provided a satisfactory answer, nor have learned criminologists.

Why have the prisons become so disproportionately black and Hispanic in the last few years? Why is their population composed of the poor?

Some will say that society in the land of plenty is hostile to poverty and those who suffer from that affliction. Amateur analysts may therefore theorize that the poor act out their hostility to the haves through larcenies, some of which are violent and fatal. Obviously, there is a criminal class. Too often to be accidental, the criminal class is a class within a class, for most who are caught and convicted belong to that underclass known as the poor. It may sound like a cliché, but it seems that society manufactures both the poor and its criminal element.

That shabby deception we know as the low-rent housing project has long been a breeding ground for crime. Sometimes crime is the only way the poor can get even with society for the housing it so grudgingly extends to them. The absence of common amenities, such as closet doors, in modern high-rise pro-

201

jects is common, even cold-water flats and old-law tenements had doors on their closets.

The constant presence of police officers in housing projects gives the poor the impression that they are being carefully watched, the way keepers in a zoo watch dangerous animals. Thus, when captured from such an environment, defendants who are poor find little difference between the jails and their homes. Indeed, poor prisoners in jail sometimes have beds all to themselves for the first time in their lives.

For ten years in the Criminal Court I watched the parade of the poor. It was my duty, I felt, to see that for once, at least, they received a fair deal and that those whites who stood before the bar got a quality of justice no different from that received by blacks and Hispanics.

To that extent, the element of race interfered with my own judgment. But to the extent that I considered race, it was to make certain that neither white nor black skin would be discriminated against in my court. I believed that the purpose of justice, among other things, was to do everything possible to make certain that a criminal defendant did not become a recidivist.

Clearly, I have been a failure. The latest statistics reveal that most of those arrested, tried, and convicted have been repeaters and persistently involved in careers of crime.

We should have learned by now that locking them up and throwing the key away is not the answer. We may throw the key away, but there is always a parole board that, by law, must review sentences after a specified term has been served. In its discretion, it can say that defendants are ready to be released into society irrespective of the loudly proclaimed Rockefeller narcotics law, which threatened to keep drug offenders in prison for life.

What this means is that an offender sentenced to life may serve from one to more years but will eventually be discharged from prison. The life sentence means only that when released, a defendant will be under the eye of a parole officer for the remainder of his life. But he will be out in the streets and not behind bars.

So fearful and alarmed has the populace become that at the process of arraignment, when a defendant is merely charged with a crime, society lusts for his blood and applauds his capture only if bail is set at an impossible and inflationary figure. They cheer the violation of the very Constitution which they say is endangered by the felons.

Most authorities who take the Eighth Amendment to the Constitution seriously agree that when the Amendment says bail shall not be excessive, it means that it must be reasonable.

What is reasonable for a person who has two dollars? All too often, the judges are concerned about a public reaction to what they do. These are the same judges who instruct a jury to disregard what public reaction may be to a verdict and not to be concerned about whether it will be popular or unpopular.

Realizing that Toryism has seized the land, a judge will not risk press and public excoriation and will fix bail at a figure guaranteed to satisfy a public mood and keep the defendant in prison before he is convicted of anything. Given that the largest number of criminal defendants are from our inner cities and black, bail becomes an instrument of social repression. In such cases the presumption of innocence is abandoned, and the judge has done what he believes the anxious public would have done had it been the judge. Thus judging becomes abandoned to the public and judicial discretion becomes whatever a judge perceives a community emotion to demand. Worse, it sometimes becomes what he believes would not offend the media.

The hard fact is that none of us knows what to do about crime, other than hope that our persons and our homes will be secure. But in our desperation to do something, we send offenders to jail.

Judges, divorced from the way of life of the streets, hear a catalog of crimes read off and charged to the defendant. They are appalled. It is not their way of life. They are shocked. They become angry. They realize that they are really a sedate security force and keepers of the peace that has been lost.

In their minds, they convict the defendant. He becomes the embodiment of the accusations against him, a grave menace and danger to society.

Some judges may think of Edwin Markham's "The Man with the Hoe," and wonder, "Who loosed and let down that brutal jaw." It is then that the judge comes to believe that there really *is* a criminal class of predators whose only mission is to prey upon both the wary and the unwary. Their language is different from that of the judicial class. They mumble out their pleas. They try to manipulate the system that has already manipulated them. They become actors in what they regard as a theater of the absurd. They put on false faces of either humility or defiance.

Their very postures dissemble. They are embarrassed not because of their public exposure, but because they have failed in their craft, and sometimes they are simply angry for being falsely accused. But for those who are as guilty as politicians trapped on videotape, the failure to defeat detection becomes the ultimate offense against themselves.

Somehow, those of us who sit in judgment suspect that the defendants are plotting to do better when they get out, that is, better at avoiding the respectable traps laid for them by society. And so, as with the juror mentioned earlier, we believe that we should just put them away "for a good long while."

Then there is the matter of recidivism. That prisoners should plot their vengeance is not surprising. The custody that is given to inspire penitence and atonement can often be brutal and inhumane. Most of New York's large prisons are in the upstate rural hinterlands. The chief industry of those areas, such as Attica, Clinton, Dannemora and Greenhaven, is custody. The deprivation of family and affectionate touching does not breed kindliness or gentility.

After years of such a hostile siege, society discharges its prisoners back to the streets from which they were captured. What have they learned in prison that fits them for a role as a model citizen? If it's making license plates, there's only one place they are made. If it is learning how to share a cell with another captive, that's not what participation in society is all about.

Discharged prisoners are expected to find a job, but doing what? Where? With communities seized by fear of crime? They do not gladly welcome ex-convicts.

There are a few federal prisons that have no walls, but do have libraries, tennis courts, swimming pools, saunas and other amenities generally associated with private country clubs. Many of the Watergate offenders seem to have prospered there, if not in morality, then in literature and post-release affluence.

Their crimes were not violent; they were not armed intruders and they were not poor or illiterate. In some respects, their prisons became university clubs. And yet, measured on a scale of civics and loyalty, their crimes were frightening for they reflected betrayal of a national trust, disloyalty and a corruption of the government they were sworn to uphold and defend. Such betrayals have the odor of treason and treachery.

Philosophically, at least, such crimes are much more serious than random larcenies and burglaries. The poor can always rationalize a theft, citing need. Other than misconceived power, the Watergate offenders, well educated, well-spoken, well-dressed, well-housed, could not justify their deeds.

Punishment without pity, urged President Nixon as he pressed for wholesale revision of criminal law codes. And yet, was it not pity that resulted in his pardon? Or was it simply the rule of the inner circle and clubbiness? Clearly, there was no punishment without pity for those sent off to the genteel and comfortable prisons. It is possible to regard such sojourns as no punishment at all. And now, all are successfully "rehabilitated." Nixon is much honored and shamelessly received his presidential pension, his free office space in a federal office building, a staff and secret service protection, and it would be surprising if the deed to his luxurious New Jersey estate differed largely from the covenants in those of William Rhenquist.

Poor minority prisoners and white ones as well are aware of such goings-on. They saw Vice President Agnew plead no contest to charges that he plotted some of his offenses in his White House office. He arrived at court in a chauffeur-driven limousine, he took his rap on the wrist and departed as he had arrived—in style. He is now a success in business and an author as well. He never served time in prison.

Can it be said that a betrayal of a national trust and confidence is more tolerantly regarded than robbery or burglary, because there is no violence or threat? *Are* we kinder to our embezzlers and frauds because, secretly, we hope they get away with their crimes and live to enjoy their fruits, perhaps on a tropical isle somewhere—since we would love to do the same thing?

From the disparity in regarding different kinds of crime to the disparity in sentencing is but a short step. And kindness to one as opposed to the other is a matter of belonging to the Club. The Robber Barons of the late 1800s and others verified their respectability by creating foundations, giving back to society a portion of what had been taken, with white collar calculation and tax benefits. Such a ploy is unavailable to the common thief.

The Watergate criminals appear to have found much prosperity in writing books and in appearances on television talk-shows. None is a "how-to" volume and some purport to be fiction. None of these men is known to have created a foundation to support a worthy charitable cause. All seem to have come by their financial rewards before the laws were passed that deprive criminal offenders of profit from their writings and divert such proceeds to the families of the victims.

The poor, then, are an underclass in the nation, and it is the poor who populate our prisons with a long-term presence. Very few rich people go to jail. Even fewer of the wealthy are executed. Some analysts believe it is because those of means can afford the best lawyers in the land. Certainly, they can afford bail and are free to consult and work with their lawyers and prepare their cases.

If rehabilitation is ever to be more than a word, it is something that must be tried with poor prisoners. Let them have swimming pools, saunas and prisons without walls. They have no money to flee to distant unaligned islands, or simply escape and risk confinement in a traditional prison. While they are there, in middle-class vacation comforts, train them for something practical, as computer programmers, key punch operators or workers in some other branch of the world according to high tech. Clearly they would not have something they were accustomed to. Even with ill-gotten gains, tennis and saunas would be priorities with poor larceners. They might just want to strike honestly for life, once freed.

Unless, of course, rehabilitation is to be officially neglected, much now needs to be done in restructuring our entire concept of prisons. Since infractions of any kind result in intramural sentences, ranging from a deprivation of rights to solitary confinement, each prisoner should be handed a printed set of the institution's rules of conduct upon entering. This might be his first lesson in conducting himself in a managed society. Often prisoners complain that they are punished for breaking rules they never knew existed. None of this is soft on crime. It is merely offering offenders a chance to become used to aid, receptive to community conduct standards, a routine they must follow outside the walls if they are not to be captured again.

Prison guards, like judges and police, must learn more than the bare essentials necessary to pass a Civil Service examination. They are hosts to the dissidents, malcontents and resisters of the system that jailed them. Their guests were not invited; they were sent. Under most circumstances they may be expected to be as bitter as crewmen shanghaied aboard an ancient sailing ship.

If the letters I receive define a mood, it is that the imprisoned writers believe they never had a fair trial and that none was even possible. Within the walls themselves, fairness is an urgency. If all that can be done to prevent recidivism is done in prison, those who leave that environment are not so dehumanized that their standards for survival are bluntly at odds with those of society on the outside.

While half-way houses are geared to aid in the transition between prison and freedom, ten years of prison life, if spent in inhumane conditions, cannot be undone in a matter of months. The humanitarian aspect must be practiced inside the prison, for the hungers that ferment in a dehumanized setting lead straight back to prison.

If this humanization is to be tried in major prisons, as it has been in specific federal ones, it means re-education of personnel as well as prisoners themselves. In New York, for example, although the prisons are in remote rural areas, most of the prisoners come from the cities. The vast majority of the custodial personnel are local people to whom custody of strangers is the principal industry. If the humanization experiment is to work, the prison guards, as well as their supervisors, need some education concerning the kind of background from which their prisoners come, including the way of life in ethnic ghettos and barrios, the historical and other factors that led to prison.

It seems strange that those who have betrayed the public trust by conduct in the nation's capital should be trusted with the comforts of luxury, not unlike their usual environment, when the poor are exposed to just the opposite—not unlike the usual circumstances that bred their way of life.

To have that way of life reinforced year after year in a prison, only hardens them the more, giving them no preparation for life after release. That it is a rude and harsh life is beyond doubt. One of the wardens of a federal country-club-type prison said he had no fear that his wards would simply walk out and escape. They knew that escape would mean recapture and commitment to a *real* prison.

The vast majority of prisons that exist today do little more than increase the census of an ever-increasing hostile underclass, channelled periodically back among (not into) society.

Sometimes, that underclass rebels within the walls and we read of prisoners taking their guards hostage and making demands in the name of humane conditions. Resolution of such confrontations has settled little except particular local crises, when a more universal and sweeping change in conditions is needed.

Such tragedies all too often overwhelm the actors and those who are held as symbols of what the prisoners regard as their oppression. The so-called Attica Massacre is one result. There, the then-governor of New York simply decided to use raw power and go in with guns blazing. The very people who, in theory at least, were to be rescued, were cut down as savagely as were the prisoners. One of the persons who prosecuted charges against the rebels has reassessed his own role and some of the things that resulted in the angry protest and its bloody conclusion. His book is entitled *Turkey Shoot*.

While that foray by the authorities with armed might may have won applause from holier-than-thou conservatives, it did nothing to change prisons. Prison reforms are a touchy subject. Too many people have been victimized by crime, one way or another.

The public feeling is one of fear. The politician, mayor, governor or legislator who urges changes is likely to forfeit the prize of his office. He will be accused of being a weeping sympathizer with criminals, a bleeding heart and soft-headed. In responding to such fears, neither the public nor the legislators appear to see that they are aiding and abetting a system that does nothing more than perpetuate the errors of old.

When Benjamin Ward was New York's Correction Commissioner, he was brave enough to introduce contact visits between married prisoners and their spouses. This, at least, allowed prisoners some semblance of family, some appreciation for the humanity they could look forward to.

Late on weekend nights at Columbus Circle in Manhattan, buses of all sizes and kind, as well as small vans, line up, and wives, children and parents of prisoners assemble to start the eight hour trips upstate to visit. They appear to be 99 percent black or Hispanic, reflecting the prison population itself.

To witness such an example of family love and loyalty makes it the more astonishing that criminals could come from such an affectionate background. It confirms, also, how many people believe firmly that the system has been unfair and unjust.

Prisoners themselves find time to issue petitions and briefs in their own cause, expressing doubts about their lawyers, assigned and otherwise. Some focus upon technicalities that might, at best, give them a new trial.

Others, and there are many, deny that they were guilty at all. One of the more remarkable things one notices from such protests is how literate former school drop-outs have become in prison. They cite and distinguish leading cases, advance theories and press writs. They appear to have learned in prison many of the disciplines they rejected when at liberty.

There is some hope to be found in the fact that several universities have brought programs within the walls, where regular instruction can be had and some degrees won. It would be helpful to know what records the prisons keep of its college graduates and how the graduates have fared, once out.

One way to bring about change would seem to be having realistic training programs for those sentenced to a period of years. First, wardens and their staff would have to discover what skills industry requires most often. Every day, for example, in classified newspaper ads, there are literally hundreds of jobs that seek qualified applicants.

After research into what is needed (for example, high tech experts are much in demand), programs could be organized around need. Then, of course, the authorities would have to persuade industry to employ ex-convicts.

It is a mammoth job, of course. If ever anything is to be done, both on the practical and experimental side, a start must be made. To do nothing is, in effect, to welcome back into the same society that bred them the former prisoners who have no prospects and only the suspicion and scorn of the public. The only recourse they have is, again, to crime, all to the public's deprivation and the taxpayer's expense.

The prominent place such attitudes hold in the judicial mind can often generate bitter hostility. In 1972, the New York City community and neighborhood lawyers representing the poor sued, seeking to have the appellate judges admonish those in the lower trial courts not to vent their hostility against the poor or against the lawyers who defended them.

Such admonitions, however, seldom undo the class antagonism frequently generated among black-robed guardians of their society's morals. When the defendant is black, all too often the judge sees before him a member of what is regarded as a nonliterate society, an enemy of the judge's own society, and perhaps a potential personal enemy.

With the power to punish at hand, the judges deem that such aliens to their way of life must be banished. It is as though there is no hope for the black, no deserved consequence other than durance vile. The enmity reserved for the poor becomes intensified when poverty is also black. It is then that Shaw's words from the preface to *Major Barbara* come alive: one can understand how "the greatest evils and the worst of crimes is poverty."

One is allowed to speculate why so many blacks and Hispanics are held in prison. The latest tabulation shows that more than 55 percent of the prisoners are black and some 13 percent are Hispanic. This probably does not take into consideration some Hispanics whose criminal records say they are "white."

One District of Columbia judge, anxious to see the places of confinement where he sent defendants, visited several jails. He was astonished, he said, because the vast majority of the prisoners were black. He said he remembered seeing numbers of whites charged with crime, and he wondered whatever happened to them because so few were detained.

It was as though society feared the black offender more than the white one and had devised different concepts of punishment for each.

It is facile to say that poverty provides fertile inspiration for crime, even when the crimes are violent and appear to have little or no connection with economic need or profit. And yet, what other explanation is available to reason, unless it be assumed that there is an underclass among us, thriving on its bloodlust?

Anthropologically, I suppose it might be said that the divisions in our society as a whole invite the exploitation of one class by the other and that it has always been that way. There have always been kings, no matter what they were called. They justify the fealty they demand by suggesting that reciprocity sustains the class arrangement. The kings protect and the other classes serve.

Maintaining such social divisions in some degree of harmony preserves the system. Those who offend such a plan are seen as disrupting the harmony, and they must be punished exemplary harshness to preserve the harmony and thus the system itself, with its advantages resting securely with one group and the disadvantages and lack of benefits imposed on the other.

It is not suggested that poor blacks analyze such a system of benefits and deprivations intellectually and decide that criminal revolution is the only way, but they must *feel* it. They know something has failed. They break a social contract that was not of their making in the first place.

There is, in fact, nothing else for them to do. The desperation of poverty, powerlessness, and hopelessness can induce a despairing recklessness that leads one to say, in effect, "What have I got to lose." Nothing, of course, and if not caught, there can be great and tax-free profit.

In such situations of tension and conflict, the morality of self-interest triumphs over any purely philosophical theory of morals, and the morality of the poor becomes distinctly different from the comfortable morality of the haves. In microcosm, we then have a breached social contract and individual revolutions against the system. Success in crime becomes the criminal's private coup d'etat, his momentary victory.

Naturally, social relationships are not supposed to be this way in a moral society. On the other hand, the poor doubtless believe that society should not be the way it is to them. Whatever has been done about crime in the past has been unavailing.

Idealists continue to attend conferences, seminars, preceptorials, and research conventions on what to do about crime. It has become a persistent mystery and one of civilization's inexplicable vexations. And so we plunge blindly on, perpetuating a system of both crime and outmoded forms of punishment.

It takes time to analyze the social processes involved in law and order and in the haves and the have-nots. Investment in such speculative hopefulness is unpopular. It is simply not the popular will. Nor is the abatement of racism in America the popular will.

If anything, there are little signs now and then that racism is encouraged. *The New York Times* for June 28, 1985, reported that a judge in Kentucky awarded worker's compensation to a white man based on the latter's "fear of working with black people."

The 39-year-old beneficiary of this largesse was said by a psychiatrist to suffer from paranoid schizophrenia. Such a precedent may open a door that might bankrupt workers' compensation funds.

It is almost as though the civil rights movement, with its passing era of goodwill and good feeling, has been re-assessed as a national mistake. Those who signed the "Southern Manifesto" have their emotional successors in Congress, and they seem to know the mood of the country as efforts proceed apace to undo some of the civil rights victories of the 1960s. At least, many view the Reagan administration as leading the way in such an about-face march.

I remain convinced that so long as Americans can see the darkness of skin color, just so long will they feel that discriminations based upon that distinction are perfectly natural and not immoral. Indeed, such discriminations are *very* American, representing a kind of genetically implanted view that is inseparable from American history.

The national preference for white skin may define a problem that is beyond solution, absent a nation of the blind. Too many of our institutions are based on exclusion of some from the blessings and benefits of our systems and its society. This creates a sub-society that must take what it wants, alas.

For some of us, theories of justice will occupy our sense of inquiry forever. Perhaps, as in the field of pure science, some ultimate discovery will be made by accident for the disease-like irritation of both crime and racism. And perhaps, just perhaps, such a discovery will promote justice as fairness, a fairness from which the taint of democracy's racism will be absent.

214